SUCCESS WITH
WATER GARDENS

SUCCESS WITH
WATER
GARDENS

Graham Clarke

GUILD OF MASTER CRAFTSMAN
PUBLICATIONS LTD

First published 2007 by
Guild of Master Craftsman Publications Ltd
Castle Place, 166 High Street
Lewes, East Sussex BN7 1XU

All the pictures were taken by the author, except for those listed below:
GMC/Anthony Bailey: 26/27, 29 (top), 39 (all), 55, 152 (top), 154.
GMC/Ed Gabriel: 10/11, 13, 14, 15 (top), 17, 25 (top left), 30, 31
(bottom), 33 (bottom), 36 (left), 37 (bottom), 42, 45, 46 (top), 84, 88.
GMC/Martin Page: 85, 87 (right), 96, 100, 101 (all), 105 (both), 109,
11, 111, 113, 117, 118, 119, 120, 122, 123, 125, 126, 130, 133
(bottom), 134 (left top and bottom), 135, 138, 139, 140 (both), 141,
142, 143, 144, 145 (bottom), 146 (all), 149, 151 (both), 152 (bottom),
153, 155. GMC/Mark Baker: 70, 71 (bottom), and illustration of leech.
GMC/Chris Skarbon: 31 (top). GMC/Christine Richardson: 78, 129
(both), 150 (top). GMC/Rob Wheele: 71 (three illustrations of newts).
GMC/Freda Cox: 8 (illustration of Ancient Egyptian garden).
The following individuals: Brian Bevan: 95. Dave Bevan: 98, 115, 121.
Eric Sawford: 114, 127. Pat Culling: 62.
Christopher Bibb: 68. Tracy Hallett: 128.
And the following companies: Hozelock Cyprio: 20/21 (illustrations), 22,
24, 29 (bottom), 35 (all), 36 (right), 38 (all), 46 (bottom), 47 (both), 51.
Harcostar: 9 (centre). Lotus: 9 (bottom). Heissner: 28. Tetra: 40 (all).
Rapitest: 49 (bottom). Trident: 72.

ISBN: 978-1-86108-523-8

Whilst every effort has been made to obtain permission from the copyright
holders for all material used in this book, the publishers will be pleased
to hear from anyone who has not been appropriately acknowledged, and
to make the correction in future reprints.

The publishers and author can accept no legal responsibility for any
consequences arising from the application of information, advice or
instructions given in this publication.

A catalogue record for this book is available from the British Library.

Production Manager: Jim Bulley
Managing Editor: Gerrie Purcell
Editor: Rachel Netherwood
Managing Art Editor: Gilda Pacitti
Designer: John Hawkins

Set in Futura
Colour origination by Altaimage
Printed and bound by Sino Publishing

Contents

LEFT **Adding the element of water to a garden, particularly moving water such as a waterfall, cascades and fountains, creates added life and interest to the setting**

ABOVE This drawing of an ancient Egyptian garden shows the importance of water, both for aesthetic and practical value

Introduction

The first decorative gardens were built in ancient Egypt and evidence shows that water has been used as an ornamental feature, as well as for the more obvious use of irrigation of crops, virtually since the beginning of recorded history.

The Egyptians dammed water to irrigate the meagre crops growing in the hot inhospitable soils, as well as to prevent and reduce the impact of the frequent flooding of the Nile. Terraces and sluices played a part, as well as man-made channels, canals and reservoirs. Humans were, for the first time, engineering the use of water.

The earliest gardeners soon recognized the potential of water as both a symbolic and decorative element, and it rapidly became a feature of the landscape and of individual gardens. What evidence do we have of this? Well, one example is that of a figurative sculpture, found by historians in Mesopotamia, and dated at around 4,000 years old. It appears to have been used as a fountain, and so could be considered to be the prototype of today's ornamental garden fountains.

Another example took place around 3,000 years ago during China's Shang dynasty, when gardens and parks incorporating water were created. The familiar black and white Yin-Yang symbol — the two opposing forces of life — were represented by water and rock.

And 2,500 years ago Islamic garden 'designers' used two intersecting canals to create a geometric garden, representing the four rivers of paradise and the elements of water, fire, air and earth.

Much has been documented about the history of water in our lives, and how it is the essential provider of life. It is just as important today, of course, but in these chaotic modern times of fast living, fast food and fast cars, water is also seen as a facilitator of peace and harmony. Think of the tranquility of either a great lake or a meandering stream. Hundreds of thousands of people take their annual vacations to visit such places, to recharge their batteries, take in the clean air and to attempt to become at one with Nature.

Many of us try to recreate a little bit of this tranquility in our own gardens, albeit on a much-reduced scale, and for most of us the appeal of a garden pond (or some such water feature) comes down to two things: first, it is an indisputable combination of beauty and serenity — two qualities that are hard to distinguish between and, for me, the one goes very much with the other.

Second, all water gardeners, no matter how 'devout', are fascinated to discover and encourage the secret hidden world that is teeming with life and interest down amongst the depths. Yes, water gardening is as much about enjoying another world, as it is about looking after fish and choosing waterlilies.

There are the more specific attributes, too, which make ponds enjoyable: the first has to be moving water — to many gardeners, the most enjoyable aspect of their pond is the sight and sound of a waterfall or fountain. Then there is the 'livestock' element, fish and assorted wildlife, which can become a near obsession to some pond owners.

My aim here is to point out to newcomers (and to remind those longer-serving water gardeners) that there are many facets to a pond. Some are rules to stick by; others are ideas to copy. But all make very good sense and most (if not all) are within anyone's capabilities.

LEFT **Rock can play a hugely important role in making an 'artificial' water feature appear to be 'natural'**

11

First decisions

Once you have decided to add a water feature to your garden, try to resist the temptation to rush out immediately and build it: unless you plan carefully, you could create all sorts of problems for the future. A good feature takes time to install, as well as a considerable amount of money and, once in situ, it cannot be moved easily. So don't risk spoiling your enjoyment of the garden and the feature itself – make sure you first consider every option fully. When incorporating water into your garden for the first time, you can treat the garden as a blank canvas and choose where the feature will go, as well as its style and size. But remember, there are four limiting factors:

- The type of garden you have: a magnificently opulent fountain would be completely out of place in an informal garden.
- Your garden's proportions: these should determine the size of the feature.
- The size of your budget: the equivalent of a week's salary or a year's!
- The level of your enthusiasm: how thoroughly you plan and execute your ideas can make all the difference to the success of your plan.

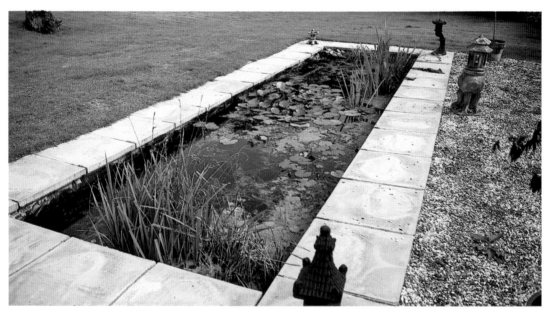

ABOVE **A straight-edged formal pond looks impressive – but would not suit every garden**

CHOOSING DESIGN AND STYLE

Water is versatile and adaptable and can be incorporated in many forms. Small features might include a barrel pond or cobblestone fountain, either of which would be ideal for a tiny town garden or patio area. Ponds, perhaps 3–6ft (1–2m) across, are what most gardeners possess, and these can be wonderful to create and nurture. At the other end of the scale you might consider a lake or large bog garden – if there is the room.

FORMAL DESIGNS

These are either circular, oval, or angular – a square, rectangle or other geometric shape. Formal ponds are particularly suitable where space is limited. They look best in more formal surroundings, for example near the house, or in conjunction with other features such as straight paths and patios. Raised or sunken ponds can add a further attractive dimension to the garden.

INFORMAL DESIGNS

By contrast, informal ponds are irregular in shape, with soft, sweeping curves and few, if any, straight lines or sharp angles. This type of design is best suited to a garden planted in a relaxed way – a sort of cottage garden, with flowers of all sizes and colours. If you like lots of plants, an informal style of pond would suit you best. For example, a bog garden can be created as an extension of the pond, making a perfect transition between the pond and garden.

STILL-WATER POND

This is the basic, unsophisticated type of pond, without a fountain or waterfall, and no mechanical filtration using pumps. This may sound rather boring, yet in many cases it is preferable if you wish to keep fish and grow a variety of aquatic plants – especially waterlilies, which hate too much moving water around their stems and leaves.

ABOVE **A water feature, such as this pump and bath, will provide sound and movement in the garden**

MOVING WATER POND

For most of us, the perfect pond is one in which there is some form of moving water. It may be the trickle of a little fountain, or a big gusher with a larger water feature; a gentle cascade over some rocks or, at the other end of the scale, a waterfall torrent. In all cases, unless your garden contains a natural waterfall, or you live on a geyser, the water will be recycled using a pump.

POND FACT

Wherever it is sited, your pond should be at least 18in (45cm) deep at some point, to prevent the water freezing completely in winter. If the surface area is 50sq ft (4.6m²) or more, and if you plan to have various types of fish, then a depth of 2ft (60cm) is better. For even larger ponds, a depth of 30in (75cm) is desirable.

FISH POND

There are two fixed rules about keeping fish in an outdoor pond:

1 The dimensions of the pond – or more accurately, the volume of water in the pond – should determine the amount and size of the fish introduced.

2 The types of fish kept must be fully hardy and not 'tender exotics', which would come to harm during a cold winter.

'Mixed pond' would be a more appropriate name than 'fish pond' for, although you would be keeping a selection of fish in it, there would undoubtedly be plants and pondweed, inevitably there would be insect life and very probably amphibians such as toads, frogs and newts. However, regardless of the eventual constituent parts of your pond, it is the keeping of fish that many gardeners enjoy. The colours, the timidity and the serenity that fish bring to the scene cannot be equalled.

ABOVE **Patio ponds are often raised, so you can sit on the side and see the water up close**

POND FACT

For a 'proper' pond, which can be expected to stay clear, you should aim for a water surface of at least 40sq ft (3.7m²). Putting in suffcient plants to cover a third of the pond surface will create the best ecological balance.

WILDLIFE POND

I conducted a survey with readers of a national gardening magazine a few years ago, and 86% maintained that their main reason for having a pond was to watch and encourage wildlife. Informal ponds make the best environments for aquatic wildlife, too. In theory, a true wildlife pond would be one that was built entirely from natural materials and contained only plants and animals native to the area. In reality, however, these preconditions are either difficult or impossible to recreate and so most wildlife ponds are artificial havens. And havens they are, for the hundreds of species which will be attracted to the pond will themselves attract other non-aquatic animals, such as birds, bees, butterflies and foxes.

RAISED POND

Any raised feature in an otherwise flat garden will add interest, but one containing water is always special. Patio ponds are often raised, so you can sit on the edge and appreciate the pond life at close quarters. It may also be the only way of having a pond if the ground cannot be excavated. If a very deep pond is required – e.g. for keeping koi – then elevating it would mean less excavation and reduce the overall costs, which could otherwise be huge. A raised pond can also be a disincentive to marauding creatures – predominately cats and herons – which can mercilessly decimate a collection of fish.

ABOVE **A small, raised water feature, including fountain**

ABOVE **A half-barrel feature with an old-fashioned water pump**

ABOVE **A purpose-made tray and water urn**

POND FACT

The minimum safe distance between a tree and a pond is that equivalent to the eventual height of the tree in question.

POND FACT

When laying flexible liners, it is always better to stick to gentle curves and simple shapes. Try to avoid sharp corners and fussiness. Both gently sloping and straight vertical sides can also cause problems, so it is better to aim for 20° sides.

CONTAINER FEATURES

Small water features which do not require an actual pond were once rare to see; today they sell in their millions and can be bought as manufactured items, or made up at home with paraphernalia accrued from all manner of sources. As long as the end result is watertight, your imagination can run riot!

A small water feature can be anything from a wall-mounted ornate reservoir, that is little more than a glorified bird bath, through to wooden barrels, Japanese bamboo bird and deer scarers and old kitchen sinks, to more sophisticated pebble and millstone fountains. These can be fairly inexpensive, quick to install, stunning to look at and a marvellous talking point. On the downside, the small size will limit the range of fish or plants you can keep in it; shade will be required for part of the day in very hot weather, to prevent the water temperature rising to dangerous levels for the water life, and regular checks will be needed to replenish water levels.

CONCLUSION

Whatever design and style you choose for your pond, avoid having too many niches, nooks and crannies, otherwise it could be a real problem to construct and look over-fussy when completed. When in doubt, always choose the simple option, as straightforward, uncomplicated shapes are usually more attractive than over-ambitious, complex designs.

THE POND SURROUND

In many cases, the pond surround is just as important to the overall appearance of the garden as the pond itself and it is important to plan the surround at the same time as the pond, otherwise the end result could be at best incongruous, and at worst, hideous. There are many styles of pond surround available, a few of which are covered here.

WOODEN DECKING

Gardeners have been a little slow to adopt the largely American, Scandinavian and Far Eastern ideas of surrounding a pond with wooden decking. But, in recent years, dozens of manufacturers have emerged to make this a popular and affordable garden feature. Decking is warmer and more comfortable underfoot than traditional paving, blends well with the garden, and is more sympathetic to the concept of the garden being a 'living space' – the fabled 'outdoor room', or 'extension of the home'.

ROCK AND PAVING

Natural and/or artificial stone can make ideal partners for a pond, whether as paving around the edge, walling to form the sides, or rock and stone to form the water feature itself. Natural quarried stone is ideal for many gardens – particularly if you want your feature to be sympathetic to the local environment – but most, particularly real slate, can be extremely expensive to buy. Artificial paving and walling (which is mostly concrete) can look very realistic, is cheaper and often simpler to lay.

BEDS AND BORDERS

These are, arguably, as natural-looking as any other style of pond surround. Plants growing over and into the water can be most appealing, especially with wildlife ponds and bog gardens, where there is often no defining line between the water and the planted areas. The key here is to allow access points at strategic places around the pond's edge, so you can get close to the water.

ABOVE **Wooden decking can provide an excellent edging to a pond and is more comfortable underfoot than paving**

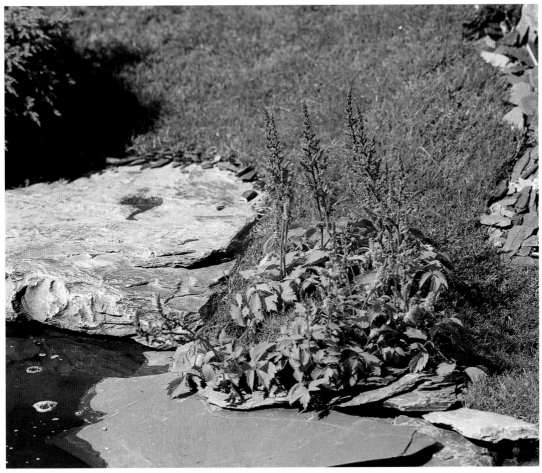

ABOVE **Do not bring the lawn right to the water's edge – the grass will be difficult to cut**

LAWNS

The least natural, and most frustrating pond surround of all is an area of maintained lawn. It is least natural because it doesn't occur in the wild – grass banks may run down to highland streams, but the grass is not maintained in an ornamental sense. I use the word 'frustrating', because, if you do cut grass close to a pond, you cannot avoid getting clippings onto the water surface.

POND FACT

When digging a hole for your pond, you can make it any shape you want, but calculating the amount of liner required becomes a nightmare. Use this formula:

Length of sheet required = pond length plus 2 x pond depth plus 2ft (60cm)

Width of sheet required = pond width, plus 2 x pond depth, plus 2ft (60cm)

WHERE TO SITE YOUR FEATURE

There are five golden rules for siting a pond.

- ◆ Choose a sunny spot, preferably sheltered from cold easterly winds. For a pond to reach its full potential in a temperate climate, for instance, it should be positioned where the sun can shine upon it for at least half the day – indeed waterlilies will only give of their best if they receive six hours or more of sunshine per day. It has to be said, however, that in very hot countries – such as the Mediterranean region and north Africa – some shade is positively beneficial!
- ◆ Avoid overhanging trees – they cast shade, and their fallen leaves will readily pollute the water with harmful salts and gases, which also encourage algae. The worst offenders are horse chestnut, laburnum, holly and – would you believe – willow, so avoid these trees if you can. Plums and cherries, meanwhile, host waterlily aphids in winter.

POND FACT
Use this guide to help you select the right thickness of liner.
Depth under 10m² (30sq ft): 0.5mm liner
Depth up to 15cm (6in): 1mm liner
Depth over 15cm (6in): 1.5mm liner

- ◆ Make sure your site is level. This makes for easier installation, a better-looking result, and will be easier to maintain.
- ◆ Choose a low-lying site, to avoid unnecessary exposure to the elements, but make sure that your chosen location is sited above the water table, otherwise flooding of the whole area will be a regular occurrence.
- ◆ Do not place a pond at the base of a slope. Run-off from the higher levels will cause problems, and places like this also act as 'frost pockets' because the average temperature of this part of the garden is lower, and so water will more readily ice over.

The following are merely recommendations for the best siting of a pond, not preconditions, like those listed above.

- ◆ Site the pond close to the house and power supplies (for running the electric pumps, filters, under-water lighting and so on).
- ◆ Ensure that the pond is clearly visible from several vantage points around the garden.
- ◆ Avoid locations with unsightly surroundings, especially those that would cast ugly reflections in the water.

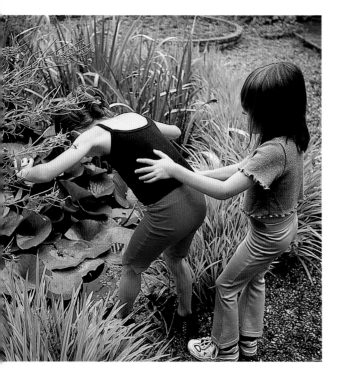

ABOVE **Any water feaure is a potential hazard if you have children**

MATERIALS

Ponds need to be watertight – to achieve this, there are three main options.

PREFABRICATED PONDS

Rigid moulded liners made from vacuum-formed plastic are the cheapest and they usually come with built-in shelves. They are relatively easy to install, and many people like them because the shape is predetermined, but they are fairly short-lived. PVC-based and rubberized compounds are available; these are slightly more expensive, but are longer lasting. Moulded fibreglass pre-formed liners are the longest lasting of all, but are more expensive and not so easy to find.

FLEXIBLE LINERS

These lengths of waterproof sheeting enable you to build a pond of any shape or size. More planning is required, and calculating the amount of liner you need is not always easy. Lined ponds are ideal for informal schemes, since the sheeting will fit most shapes and contours, albeit with varying amounts of creasing. The most reliable liner is rubber sheeting known as butyl, but PVC and LDPE (low-density polyethylene) sheets are also recommended. Buy lengths with a guarantee of 20 years or more.

CONCRETE PONDS

Concrete was the main choice years ago, but is no longer favoured. Achieving the right mix, applying it correctly and keeping it workable, are tasks that many beginners get wrong. Yet, properly designed and constructed, a concrete pond can be elegant and have an air of permanence unequalled by other materials.

SAFETY

Safety must be paramount at all times, as any water feature is a potential hazard. If a pond is big enough for plants and fish, chances are it is also big enough for a child to fall in. So safety must be a major consideration if children are

likely to be present. Choose a site with all-round visibility, so that you can keep an eye on children while they are playing in the vicinity.

Barrier fencing is an obvious safety measure, and it need not be unsightly. Picket fencing is certainly an effective barrier (and can look quite attractive, too) but it must be at least 30in (75cm) high. Both metal hoop fencing as used in parks, and chain link fencing as used around school playgrounds, will merge into the background greenery and be less obtrusive if painted dark green. Heavy grilles placed over the pond might save lighter children from taking a dip, but this is hardly an attractive feature.

The barriers mentioned above will also protect your fish from cats and herons. But as far as children are concerned, if your pond poses a permanent risk to them it is better to be without it until they reach an age when you do not have to watch them constantly.

ABOVE **Ponds made from rigid, moulded lines usually come with built-in shelves**

POND FACT
Herons will gobble up a pond's stock of fish but will also eat small mammals, reptiles, insects, worms and even small birds. Dawn and dusk are the favoured times for eating.

CHAPTER 2

How to start

There are, of course, many ways of featuring water in a garden so it is crucial to establish at the outset the type of feature that you want.

Essentially there are three general types:

♦ Feature with moving water (fountain, cascade, stream)
♦ Still pond for fish and wildlife (and plants)
♦ Self-contained water container (barrel, wall fountain, raised pond)

Whichever feature you choose, consider very carefully how best it can be designed into the context of your garden so that it feels and looks right. In this way you will ensure that the feature – and therefore the whole garden – is pleasing aesthetically.

Firstly, decide on the mood or style of your feature, and how it will eventually look as part of the overall garden: it could, for instance, be an informal design, with curving sides and associated planting to make a natural setting. Alternatively it could be very formal, comprising a water feature with lots of straight edges and very little planting.

COMMITTING TO PAPER

If you are planning a feature that is more complex than a simple hole in the ground filled with water, then it would be wise to produce a scale drawing or plan of the area. This must include all of the garden's 'fixtures and fittings', i.e. the house, greenhouse/shed, immovable and desirable trees and shrubs, paths/ driveways, paving and walling, drains and sewers, electricity poles and so on. Consider also whether you might want to extend your home at some stage in the future; it would be a shame and a great waste of time, effort and money, to install a major water feature only to dig it out later when an extension is built.

ABOVE **Cross section of a small pond and fountain**

ABOVE **Similar pond with pump and circulating cascade**

It is tempting to try to minimize the overall effort when designing a water feature, but it may be necessary to alter or move fixtures to accommodate it, so don't compromise the garden just to save on effort. If the pond really needs to go where the greenhouse is currently sited, and there is somewhere else for the greenhouse to go, then do it.

The best way to start a paper plan is to conduct your own 'survey' of the garden. Walk around the house (and any fixed outbuildings) and make a large sketch of the layout, in plan form but not necessarily to scale.

A long, flexible measuring tape is useful, and a good starting point is a particular part of the house, say the back door. Measure the distance from the door to your proposed water feature. This gives you a mental picture of distance combined with an actual measurement.

Then you can prepare several plans, each incorporating a pond of a different shape and size, located at different points within your garden scheme, but always in accordance with the rules of where not to site a pond. If you don't want to prepare a new garden plan for each design, simply produce one and move cut-outs of different shaped and sized ponds within the layout until you are happy with a particular grouping. If you have a computer there are some excellent garden design software packages that offer much versatility in drafting a plan.

ABOVE **Avoid placing a pond under overhanging trees**

The final act, prior to acquisition and construction, is to lay a hosepipe on the ground to form the outline of your proposed pond site. Few people bother to do this, but it can resolve a number of issues and avoid future regrets. Live with this for a few days – before you embark on any excavation work. You will then be able to make adjustments, and satisfy yourself that this is absolutely the best place, the best size and the best shape for your water feature.

ABOVE **Some pumps can run fountains and cascades together**

ABOVE **Cross section of a small pebble fountain**

EXCAVATION AND INSTALLATION

The first thing that any gardener planning to reconstruct a garden should be aware of, particularly if they are undertaking much of the construction work themselves, is that the whole project should be fun.

If you are planning to employ professional landscapers or builders to do the 'heavy' part of your garden construction it is always important to get several estimates for work to be carried out. Professionals are likely to work outside in all weathers but, if you're doing it yourself, you have the luxury of picking and choosing when to do the work.

Nobody really likes the idea of their garden turning into a building site but, if the job involves a lot of concrete work, such as the building of walls and patios – or even that of the pond itself – then it is probably inevitable.

Site clearance is, arguably, the most fundamental aspect to garden reconstruction. It may involve simply shouting at the dog to get out of the way, or it might require a degree of demolition, lifting and disposal of slabs and the hiring of the ubiquitous skip (this latter operation can be quite costly, so only hire one when there is a genuine need).

POND FACT
Any drawn plan of your proposed water feature must be large enough to accommodate all of the 'fixtures' within 20ft (6m) of it.

The trees that you want to keep can hardly be called obstacles, but in some ways that is what they are. In addition, be aware of hidden obstacles, such as well-heads, drains and drainage pipes, manhole covers, electric cabling and assorted lumps of concrete hidden just under the soil.

Then you will need to mark out the site and it is crucial to know exactly where any walls are to be built and paths laid. Even a few inches out in any direction can cause big problems (especially with more intricate designs).

Thin lines of white spray paint can be used to mark bare soil and pegs, and taut string can be employed to indicate heights of walls and eventual paths. A good, old-fashioned spade should be used to mark out shallow trenches for such things as the water feature.

ABOVE **Many manufacturers make and supply a range of pre-formed ponds to meet the needs of most first-time water gardeners**

INSTALLING A PREFABRICATED POND

With this type of pond, the excavation of the hole into which the prefabricated unit will sit is crucial. If your chosen pond is a regular or symmetrically shaped unit (square, circle, rectangle, oval, etc), turn the unit upside down, and position it directly over the precise place you want the finished pond to be. With a stick, spade, or handfuls of sand, mark an outline right around the rim of the unit, but bring the mark out from the edge by about 6in (15cm). This extra space will allow for miscalculations in digging and, just as importantly, will permit backfilling later with soft soil or sand.

If your chosen pond is informal rather than symmetrical (such as the most popular kidney-shaped style), then upturning and marking out as described above will not work. Instead, place the unit upright over its intended position, and level it out with supports. Insert vertical stakes or canes in the ground at intervals all the way around, then remove the unit, and measure the depth and size of any shelves that are moulded in to it. Now with your spade, dig a level, flat-bottomed hole as marked out, but only dig to a depth just a little deeper than the level of the first shelf. Rake over the bottom of the hole and then stand the pond unit inside the hole and press down so that when you remove it again, you will see that the deeper section of the unit has left an impression.

Remove the unit again and excavate the newly marked section down to about 4in (10cm) below where the bottom of the pond will be. Always check that the pond is sitting horizontally by using a straight-edged board and a spirit level. Check in six or seven directions, to ensure that the hole is being dug with a level base. There is nothing worse than a lopsided pond.

Now check the hole thoroughly, removing any large or sharp stones. Compact the soil, and then spread a 2in (5cm) layer of builders' sand on to the base. Lower the pond gently into position, and add or take away sand until you are happy with the level. Keep checking with the spirit level. If you have measured correctly, the lip of the pond should end up lying just below ground level.

Next comes the satisfying bit – running water into the unit for the first time. But ensure you don't fill the whole pond. Run just a few inches into the bottom to stabilize the unit and to bed the bottom of it on to the sand base. Then fill in some of the larger gaps around the edge of the pond unit with sieved soil or builder's sand.

Fill to about 4in (10cm) from the lip of the pond. This will allow you room to complete your job, which may be to plant perennials or bog plants along the edge of the pond, or to lay paving stones.

ABOVE **Late winter is the best time to dig out a new pond**

POND FACT

When backfilling the sides of a pre-fabricated pond during installation, match the height of the backfilled soil or sand with the height and level of the water filling the inside of the pond. This prevents buckling of the side walls.

INSTALLING A LINED POND

Before you dig the hole for the pond, go around the outside of the proposed pond site, removing a thin layer of turf or topsoil, about 18in (45cm) wide, with a spade. This strip will form the edge of the pond, onto which the flexible liner will overlap, and over which the pond edging – paving slabs, bricks, etc – will be placed.

Dig the rest of the hole. With this type of pond the sides can slope to almost any angle from 70° to 0° (i.e. a gently sloping pond or homemade 'beach'). The shallower the slope, the better it is for wildlife. Shape the shelves as you dig down, allowing enough width – 12in (30cm) minimum – for standing planted aquatic baskets.

If your soil is very sandy or loose, it is advisable to install a supporting back wall to the top shelf, to prevent damage to the edge once the pond is in use. This can be done by lining the back of the shelf with brick or building blocks and cementing them in place.

As excavation proceeds, keep checking with a spirit level to ensure that the shelves are horizontal. Unless you want to place planted containers there, it is not so important for the bottom of the pond to be absolutely level.

Before laying the butyl or rubber liner, you should provide an 'underlay', e.g. a layer of builders' sand some 2in (5cm) thick, so the excavation should be deeper by this amount to accommodate it. Pre-made underlays consist of strips of old carpet, or proprietary underlay felt. Remove any sharp stones or boulders and position the underlay.

Installing the liner is not difficult. The easiest way is to mould the liner into the excavation, smoothing out as many creases as you can. Then run a hose into the deepest part, adjusting any folds that occur as it fills.

Once the pond is full, trim the edges of the liner, leaving sufficient width all round to form a good overlap – this will eventually be covered by the edging or surround of your choice.

CONSTRUCTING A CONCRETE POND

It takes weeks to construct a concrete pond, rather than a mere day or two as for the alternative methods. What makes concrete a realistic option however is its longevity: if made well, it will almost certainly outlast either rigid or flexible liner ponds.

Begin by marking out and digging the hole, making it about 6in (15cm) deeper and wider than the finished desired size. Shape any shelves and firm the surface of the soil so that there are few loose fragments. Ensure that the sides are no steeper than 45°, otherwise you will not be able to prevent the wet concrete from sliding to the bottom of the slope.

If your garden soil is heavy clay, you should line the hole with a 3in (8cm) layer of moist builders' sand. If you live on a sandy soil this stage can be ignored.

ABOVE **Pond liners are available in rolls or pre-cut packs**

POND FACT
Warm weather will make flexible liners more flexible and easier to handle. So, if possible, unroll the liner and leave it in the sun for about 30 minutes before using.

ABOVE **Small water features, such as this self-contained pebble fountain, are ideal for small gardens**

ABOVE **Concrete ponds take several days to construct, but they are more durable than any other kind of liner**

Next, line the hole with a 2in (5cm) thick base layer of concrete. Although it is possible to build the whole pond using one strength of concrete, a far stronger and more durable pond will be created if you adjust the ratios. Ideally, there should be three stages. The first stage – the base layer – should be mixed to the following recipe: seven parts ¾in (15mm) gravel; three parts builders' sand; one part cement. Measure the ingredients dry, with a shovel or bucket.

Always mix the concrete as near to the pond site as possible, on a hard surface such as paving or a large board. The concrete consistency should be stiff, but moist. Weak joints may be created if you add a new layer to a previous layer that has not set properly, so plan to complete each layer in a day and allow it to harden and dry overnight.

Start by lining the hole with the base layer. An hour or so after you have finished the layer, use a stiff broom to brush the drying surface, and so create a rough key for the next layer. Leave to dry overnight. Next day, cover the base layer with 2in (5cm) mesh wire netting.

This will reinforce the concrete. Overlap the strips of wire by about 4in (10cm) and tread it into place, using your feet to mould it into the contours of the pond.

Next, mix and lay another lining of concrete, but this time make it about 4in (10cm) thick, and make it to the following recipe: three parts ¾in (15mm) gravel; two parts builders' sand; one part cement, plus optional waterproofing agent to bind the mixture together. Smooth the edges with a builder's trowel, protect the surface from strong sunlight (with sacking or horticultural fleece) and leave it to set for a couple of weeks. In really hot weather it is advisable to damp it down using a watering can.

Finally, spread a 2in (5cm) thick top layer over the whole area. This should be made to the following recipe: four parts builders' sand; one part cement, plus waterproofing agent. Leave to set for a couple of weeks.

Once the final layer of concrete has set hard, coat it with a waterproofing primer and sealant, and leave it to dry. Sweep the interior of the pond prior to filling with water.

CONSTRUCTING WALLS

Many water features make use of walls. Raised ponds need low walls to support the weight and volume of water. Wall-mounted fountains (like the ubiquitous lion's head) speak for themselves.

Good, deep foundations are the key to a robust wall and that means digging a trench at least 2ft (60cm) deep. This will allow for 18in (45cm) of concrete for the main foundation, and a further 6in (15cm) for the first course of bricks to remain below ground level.

Use wooden pegs hammered into the ground and a builder's line – or some string tied to sticks – to mark out the eventual position of the wall and use this as a guide to excavate the foundations. The trench should be roughly twice as wide as the width of the wall it will support.

The foundation material is basically a concrete mix poured in to the trench. For small walls you can use a ready-to-use powder that is poured dry into the trench, then packed down, smoothed off and watered. It will set rock hard within half an hour or so. It is probably not as strong as concrete, but easier for smaller jobs.

For larger walls, the foundation mix should be concrete. Work an amount sufficient to fill a single wheelbarrow at a time, otherwise it may harden before it is all used. Mix one part cement to six parts aggregate, ballast or sharp sand. Add little amounts of water gradually, until you

reach a consistency similar to gloss paint. Too much water will require more cement/ballast which can be wasteful. Start pouring the mix into the trench. If the new wall will adjoin an existing one then start from that end.

Use a spirit level and a bit of old wood with a straight edge to tamp down and flatten the concrete, so that the final level is at just the right height for the first course of bricks or blocks. The foundation mix will harden sufficiently overnight in summer, or over a couple of days in winter.

BRICKWORK

Most garden walls are built with modern lightweight Celcon or Toplite blocks which have superseded breeze blocks and are cheaper than bricks. Heavier and sturdier walls can be achieved with the use of 'concrete' blocks. These are, however, more difficult to cut and transport around the garden. For a smaller wall use ordinary bricks, which can be laid in small spaces and won't need to be cut. Brick prices rise steeply with the better-made and designed display bricks. Use pegs and a builder's line to mark out the position of the 'face' of the wall (the side of the wall that will be most visible); this should follow a straight line, unless there is a designed curve.

It's now time to start bricklaying. Mix your mortar from one part cement to six parts soft

ABOVE **A concrete mixer will save time and is relatively cheap to hire**

ABOVE **The site should be marked out before you start digging**

ABOVE **Wall foundations should be 18in (45cm) deep with room for the first brick course to be underground**

ABOVE **Ordinary bricks should be used for the bottom few courses, or for smaller walls**

ABOVE **Build up the courses of bricks. After six courses step back and clean up the mortar**

ABOVE **Lightweight Celcon or Toplite blocks are cheaper than bricks and perfect for walls that are to be rendered**

POND FACT

If a concrete pond has been well sealed, no toxins should leach out from the concrete. Use a pH test kit, after filling the pond with water, to check its acidity/alkalinity levels. Over pH8.5 indicates a high lime content. Neutralize by adding potassium permanganate, which will initially turn the water a light pinkish colour, and leave for a few days. Pump the water out of the pond, rinse the sides and base thoroughly, refill with clean water and re-test. Leave for about six weeks before introducing any fish.

sand, or buy a ready-made mix from a DIY store. Work one wheelbarrow load at a time and, if the weather is hot, cover the mix with a sheet of plastic or wood to stop the mortar from drying out too quickly.

Begin by trowelling a ½in (1cm) layer of mortar on to the footing. Then, using your line as a guide, and checking every so often with a spirit level, start bedding in the first course of bricks.

If the first brick is to butt up to an existing wall, then its ends will need to be 'buttered'. To do this, hold the brick in one hand, trowel on a small amount of mortar, and then roughly shape it so that the mortar is at its thickest in the middle, sloping off to both sides. Then lay the brick lengthways, with the buttered end touching the bricks of the wall. Tamp the brick down on to the mortar bed and check that the brick is lined up with a spirit level in 90° directions.

Lay brick after brick, course after course then, after about six courses, step back and start cleaning up the mortar, which should be stiff enough to work. First use a jointing iron, or the bend in a piece of ½in (1cm) copper pipe, to smooth a nice clean finish between each course, then brush off the small blobs of semi-dry mortar with a soft hand brush.

THE ELECTRICS

If you want garden lighting, or to run a fountain or a waterfall in your pond, then you will need to supply power. The whole subject of electricity and electrical safety must be treated with great caution. There are big differences between wiring inside the house and wiring anywhere in the garden. Outdoor electric wiring is much more likely to get damaged than wiring hidden inside the walls, floor or roof of a house. Classic examples are cutting through a flex with a hedge trimmer or lawnmower or digging into (and perhaps through) a buried cable with a sharp spade. And, as we all know, water and electricity do not mix.

Let's be clear about the different safety measures which apply to electric wiring. The most familiar is probably fusing – but its function is to protect the wiring, not you: in particular, fusing prevents wiring overheating and potentially catching fire. A big fuse protects the whole house (and all the circuits); medium-sized fuses protect individual circuits; small fuses (such as in a plug) protect the flex leading to electrical appliances. What does help to protect you with appliances that have metal casings is 'earthing'. For example, a loose live wire inside could cause the casing to become live and give you a shock. If an appliance is earthed, the metal casing is connected to the earth wire in the plug. If a live wire does touch it, a short circuit is caused; this blows at least one of the fuses, thus protecting you from an electric shock. But this doesn't really apply in the garden, as outdoor electrical equipment is invariably non-earthed with a plastic, non-electric current carrying casing: this is called 'double insulation'.

RESIDUAL CURRENT DEVICES (RCDS)

What makes electricity dangerous to you in the garden is that you could provide a perfect earth connection if you touch a live wire – particularly if you are standing on damp ground – and the short circuit passing through you could be fatal.

This is where residual current protection comes in. A residual current device (RCD) monitors the currents flowing in the live and neutral wires of a flex or cable and acts like a switch to cut off the electrical supply if it detects even a tiny difference (perhaps because some of the current is trying to flow through you).

RCDs have saved the lives of people who have, for example, cut through the flex of a lawnmower. An RCD should therefore always be used with outside electrics.

The RCD can be in the plug used to wire an appliance, in an adaptor fitted between the plug and the socket, in the socket, on the circuit that supplies the garden, on all socket outlet circuits in the house and garden or protecting the whole house. Having a single RCD to protect the whole house sounds like the best idea, but it isn't: what is known as 'nuisance tripping' can mean that frozen food in a freezer can be ruined if the RCD trips whilst you are on holiday; if you trip a whole-house RCD when using an appliance, all the lights will go out and you could be plunged into darkness.

Some water garden suppliers have RCDs in part of their range, whilst whole-house and circuit RCDs are also made by electrical accessory manufacturers.

ABOVE **Pond pumps, along with lighting, filters and even pond vacuums, are all powered electrically**

ABOVE **Home gardeners should always use RCDs for safety reasons, but professional landscapers must use durable transformers**

LOW-VOLTAGE GARDEN CIRCUITS

Much of the electric wiring you will have in or around your pond is likely to be low voltage. That is, run at a safe 12 or 24 volts from a transformer. Only the transformer needs be connected to mains electricity; the low-voltage cable, which runs to the pond lights or to a low-voltage pond pump, can then be run along the surface of the ground without posing any danger. Legislation in many countries now requires electrical items such as pond lights to be low voltage. Some transformers are designed to be used outside and, if waterproof, even in the pond itself. If not, they must be used either inside the house or in a garden shed or other outbuilding

ABOVE **It is essential that all electrical junction boxes and connectors are waterproof and made for outdoor use**

with the low-voltage cable run outside. The problem that arises with a low-voltage circuit is how to run the cable from the house or other outbuilding and into the pond. The simplest way to get it out of the house, is to drill a hole in a convenient window frame, pass the cable through and then seal the hole with a matching silicone sealant or building mastic. To get it into the pond, you can simply pass it in behind some of the surrounding stones, or buy the special watertight cable lead-outs which some manufacturers make specifically for passing cable through walls.

MAINS-VOLTAGE GARDEN CIRCUITS

Serious pond owners will want a permanent outside electric circuit. This must always be installed by a professional electrician to comply with Building Regulations. Such a circuit should have its cable buried in the ground deep enough to avoid being severed by digging with a spade, i.e. at least two spits deep. It is possible to use normal house wiring cable for this, but it must be protected by a rigid PVC conduit. The alternative is proper armoured cable, available through DIY stores and electrical retailers, which requires special fittings for the termination at either end. External sockets are also available, which have their own special plugs.

The alternative is a junction box with up to six outlets, available from water garden suppliers. They can either be switched or unswitched (a separate switch serves each outlet).

JOINING CABLE

If for any reason you need to join mains electric cable in the garden, you must make sure that you have the right type of connector, i.e. weatherproof or waterproof. The non-weatherproof kind is only suitable for use indoors and should not be considered for anything to do with the garden.

29

CHAPTER 3

Adding features

ABOVE **The sound of moving water can even help to mask the noise of nearby traffic**

Water that is moving, whether spurting, trickling, cascading or plummeting, is one of the great joys of pond-keeping. There are small contrivances that can be added such as spurting frogs, millstones, lions' heads and even peeing urchins. And then of course there are the larger features requiring the movement of a greater water volume, such as streams, waterfalls, 'hole-in-the-wall' falls, cascades and fountains.

In many cases, sound is as important as the visual effect. There is little doubt that the sound of moving water can appear to have a cooling effect on a hot patio, and some even claim that it can mask – or partly mask – the noise of traffic from a busy nearby road. But in order to 'move' water, we must invest in a pump or two (or more, if the volume of water to be moved, or the distances involved, are considerable).

The thought of a softly falling waterfall on a sunny day is hugely appealing, but there is an even more fundamental reason why it is a good idea to have a waterfall, fountain, or cascade and that is because it helps to oxygenate the pond. This is essential if the pond is to be its own ecosystem, supporting wildlife, fish and plants. But, if your fountain spurt is barely more than an ooze, or your waterfall no more than a trickle, then your pump is too small. And conversely, if the water emanating from your drilled urn is more like a burst water main, then the pump is too large.

There are dozens of pump styles, makes and sizes available (see pages 46–47), but the general rule in determining the size of pump required is that it should circulate in one hour a volume of water equivalent to that within the pond system. All pump packs state the circulation volume per hour.

WATERFALLS

A waterfall can be made to spill gently over a shallow sill, or to gush in torrents over a high ledge, depending on its design and construction. (If the water does not free-fall and is merely tipping and tumbling over rocks, then it is not a waterfall at all, but a 'cascade' – for this see pages 32–34.)

A good waterfall is a strong statement: it dominates its setting and can easily overwhelm other features. Unfortunately, it is all too easy to miscalculate the water flow, and you can readily end up with a torrent of water crashing from a wide ledge into a tiny pond or, conversely, a tiny trickle into a huge pond. Either will look completely incongruous.

There are prefabricated, moulded units available to act as the 'header' to a waterfall, and these are simple to install. Ensure that they are level from side to side, and that the lip protrudes sufficiently over the pond – and at a suitable height – to enable a body of water to fall into the pond rather than onto the surrounding ground. The hosepipe linking the pump to the header pool should also be carefully hidden.

Sometimes moulded header units are not the right shape or size, in which case it is possible to make the waterfall from concrete and cover it with flat stone or rock, to make it look natural. Some experts recommend using flexible liners over pre-dug ground, to follow the contours of your waterfall feature but, while this is possible, it certainly is not easy. Making a feature out of concrete is more straightforward, and should also be longer lasting.

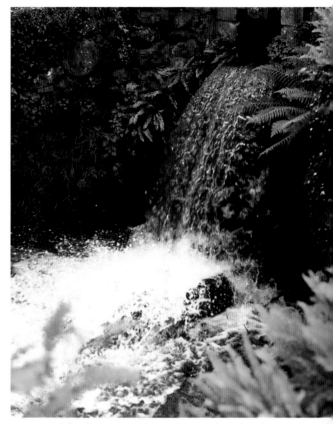

ABOVE **A waterfall makes a strong statement in any garden and a 'gusher' never fails to impress**

ABOVE **Garden caves or grottoes make a spectacular feature and may be home to shade-loving ferns**

31

If making your own header pool from concrete, use any of the same mix recipes as for the concrete pool (see pages 24–25). Ensure that the header pool itself is some 6in (15cm) deep. This isn't deep enough to support fish or plant life, but is deep enough for water to remain within the depression, even during hot weather.

A more natural effect can be created by adding the edging and base stone while the concrete is still damp. Crucially, the edges must be raised and level in the horizontal plane so that water is distributed evenly throughout the basin.

THE GROTTO WATERFALL
For this distinctive waterfall, water emits from a fairly high header basin and falls directly in front of some sort of cavern. This cavern can be easily created with concrete. Once established, it can be a haven for amphibious wildlife, as well as natural ferns and lichens. Alternatively, by installing the pump and outlet within the recesses of the cavern, and by raising the cavern level, you can give the illusion that the water is coming out of the cavern and falling into the pond.

CASCADES
The archetypal definition of a cascade is a small stream, purposefully tumbling over rocks, boulders and pebbles on its downward journey, into a pool at the bottom of a slope. With the cascade itself comes the delicate sound of water splashing, trickling and gurgling, so creating an aura of tranquility.

Most garden cascades are modelled so that they appear to be natural, but modern and contemporary equivalents, using sheets of glass, stainless steel and wooden channels, are becoming more popular.

Prefabricated sections for cascades are available from most large garden centres in kit form. Some can be made from thin, lightweight concrete and are fairly natural-looking, whilst others are made from shiny fibreglass or plastic. Although these latter sections are convenient to install, it is almost impossible to make them appear 'natural'. These artificial cascade units can either be bought as a short, self-contained header pool or cascade, or as several units which fit together to make up longer courses.

ABOVE **This cascade features water gently flowing from a hidden source into a pool**

ABOVE **A pond is the source for this cascade, which flows into a stream**

ABOVE **This style of cascade could also be referred to as a 'water staircase'**

Even though these artificial units come, more or less, as ready-made cascades, you will certainly have to spend some time on preparation work if the whole thing is to look authentic.

A domestic garden cascade can be fairly vertical, with a series of rocks protruding from each other forming the water course, to a shallow nearly level course, where the water appears more as a stream.

In practically every way, a cascade should be treated as if it were a waterfall, even though there is no significant free-falling of water.

A WATER STAIRCASE

French and Italian designers in centuries past made great use of the 'water staircase', by using lengths of concrete drainage pipe, or some such, set in a bed of concrete. Each succeeding length of pipe is set below and slightly out from its predecessor thus forming a staircase with rounded steps, down which sparkling, silvery water will tumble. Disguise the ends of the pipes with rocks or plants. This type of feature works best if there is sufficient water flowing over it, so do not skimp on the size of pump.

FOUNTAINS

Until fairly recently, most garden fountains were simple patterned sprays of water emerging from a pool. Now there are many options, ranging from sophisticated, grand affairs to small-scale child-safe features.

On the following pages I have made a selection of modern alternatives, together with some simple rules which must be followed if the chosen fountain is to be successful.

ABOVE **A 'standard' fountain – but there are many styles of water jet to choose from**

POND FACT

To calculate the volume of water in your pond, measure the length, width and depth of the pond in feet and multiply these together. Multiply the result by 6.25 to give the volume in gallons.

WALL-MOUNTED LION'S HEAD

This is usually cast into a block, made from concrete or reconstituted stone. A small pipe feeds water through the back and into the mouth, so this needs to be built into a backing wall from the outset. Water then pours either directly into a pool below or into a small suspended reservoir.

ABOVE **Two-tier fountain**

ABOVE **Three-tier fountain**

ABOVE **Bell, or sheet fountain**

ABOVE **Variable calyx-style fountain**

ABOVE **Geyser fountain**

ABOVE **Tulip-style fountain**

ABOVE This lion's head fountain is set to spurt water into a trough

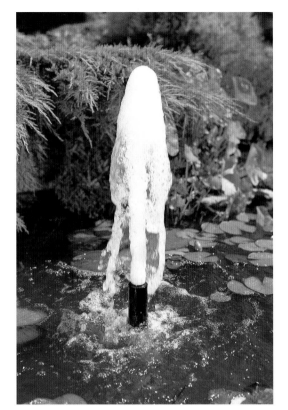

ABOVE Geyser-style fountains move a high volume of water

This can then overflow into a larger pool below, or be recirculated. Be aware that the smaller the reservoir, the greater the danger of it running dry, through evaporation, in hot weather.

GEYSER 'FOAM' JETS

These are designed to suck in air and mix it with the water to produce a lively column of foaming water which, with an appropriate pump and nozzle, can reach a height of 3ft (1m) or more.

'BELL' JETS

These compress a flow of water from a nozzle, deflecting it outwards and downwards to produce a glassy 'mushroom' of water. Lighting can produce dramatic results with this type of fountain, but you must make sure that the pond water is not dirty or full of debris.

SOLAR-POWERED FOUNTAINS

These are now becoming widely available, and more efficient. Their output is not always as good or as substantial as conventional fountains and pumps, but this technology does make it possible to have a modest fountain in a place to where it is difficult to run electricity.

BUBBLING STONES, MILLSTONES AND 'BOULDER' FOUNTAINS

In most cases these are suspended by means of a strong steel grid – sometimes with pebbles and/or rocks – over an underground tank of water. Kits are available from most large garden centres. They include a small plastic reservoir and a plastic cover with a central hole for a fountain on a submersible pump below. Check the water level in the reservoir in hot weather.

ABOVE Small fountains splashing and bubbling onto a pebble base are easy to install

ABOVE A bell fountain requires clean water – a pond containing green water will form a green 'bell', if it works at all

INSTALLING A PEBBLE FOUNTAIN

1 With a spade, make a hole in which to fit the reservoir.

2 Line the hole with sand and place the reservoir into position, ensuring it is level.

3 Place the pump housing and nozzle and fill with water.

4 Arrange washed pebbles over the pump housing platform.

5 Surround the area with plants and paving – and switch on!

INSTALLING AN EGG-STYLE FOUNTAIN

If you would prefer to see a piece of modern 'art' – something that would be both a focal point and a talking point – this smooth, high density concrete egg fountain has a timeless, contemporary feel. Dimensions of the egg stone are: height 19¾in (50cm); width 15in (38cm) and weight 176lb (80kg).

1 Excavations are started for housing the fountain 'liner' or 'reservoir'. A layer of builders' sand is required in the base of the hole in order to protect the liner from sharp stones.

2 The liner is placed in to the hole to check for depth and level – a spirit level is crucial.

3 More sand is required to protect the sides and lips of the liner, and all edge levels should be checked. The liner is finally put into position, level checked and then more sand used to in-fill and pack the sides.

4 Rubber tubing, which is cut to fit, needs to be threaded through the egg fountain and then connected to the pump.

5 The egg is placed into position, and a final check for levels is made.

6 Pebbles are placed over the inspection cover to complete the effect, and new plants surround the whole structure.

7 Within just a few weeks, the area looks established.

CONTAINERS

Water barrels, pots, urns, tubs, baths, vases and so on, whether self-contained units or linked to a larger pond, really add a different dimension to the garden. Any container that can hold water is a potential above-ground pond but it should, of course, be ornamental and decorative. For relatively little outlay, a container water feature can become a real talking point.

These containers can be placed almost anywhere in the garden but, because they are small in comparison with a whole pond, it makes sense to site them near a sitting area, or where people will spend an amount of time: on a patio, path, or close to house windows would be suitable sites. Placed to brighten up a dull corner, they can make perfect alternatives to pots of annuals and conifers.

The most important factor is that of light, particularly if you're anticipating growing flowering water plants such as waterlilies. Do not site the container in a dark corner; nor should it be in full sun for the hottest part of the year, or evaporation will be a problem.

Another factor is that of running power out to the container (in the case of those with fountains or other forms of running water), for you will need a pump. Such water containers can, of course, also be still.

Many of the metal, plastic or ceramic containers will be watertight, but water barrels – or more correctly half-barrels – could well be authentic old-style barrels made by coopers, where open air exists between the wood slats. In this case, we need to use a PVC liner.

CREATE A STILL WATER BARREL

1 Line the container with butyl or rubber sheeting.
2 & 3 Staple it in position.
4 With sharp scissors trim away the surplus.
5 Fill the barrel with water.
6 Add small aquatic plants, or a pump at this stage if required.
7 In a week or two the barrel will appear established.

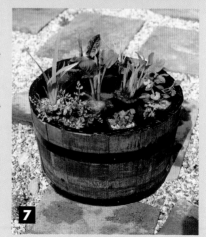

STREAMS

Most of us want our water features to look 'natural', but ponds often need to go against walls, or next to (or indeed on) patios: hardly 'natural' settings. But a garden stream can look really natural. Even though it is merely a stretch of water going from one place to another, this is exactly the sort of phenomenon that is found in the wild.

In all cases, of course, a man-made stream will contain water that is circulated by a pump. Pumps obviously vary hugely in their performance, and it is crucial that you choose one that will provide the desired effect. For example, a small pump in a very wide or deep stream would produce an imperceptible and completely ineffective flow.

The stream should be made dead level, so that it remains full once the pump is switched off. And, when the pump is off, your 'stream' will become a shallow, elongated pond.

One of the trickiest decisions when creating a stream is how to make it suddenly 'appear' in the garden, and then 'disappear' further along. A gurgling stream usually ends up emanating from large pipes or from beneath a stone slab; it will almost certainly disappear in the same way. Most of the gullies the water will travel along are made from concrete, stone or brick, and are either straight or gently curving. Flexible liner can be used, but use gravel, sand, stones, bricks or boulders to give the water a rippling texture and conceal the shiny PVC or plastic.

If an abrupt change of direction is required some way along the stream, it is best to cover the stream at that point with some sort of chamber, so that water can enter it from one direction and leave in another. Such a chamber could also be used to hide the beginning or end of the stream.

RIGHT **Garden streams can be made to look entirely natural**

STEPPING STONES

As most (human) visitors to a pond will stand on the edge and look towards the other side, across the surface of the water, one can miss beauty and activity practically at one's feet. Stepping stones can change all that: from here one can look back towards the pond edge.

Whilst stepping stones are generally meant for access across the pond, and so are designed to be in more or less a straight line, a useful design trick is to cluster a few of them in order to provide a better viewing (and maintenance) platform.

If the size of your pond allows, go for large stones that you can stand on with both feet or, even better, that you can crouch or kneel on. This will enable you to enjoy the pond at close quarters for a longer time.

POND FACT

When choosing the hosepipe to circulate water from your pump, it is important to choose one with the correct diameter, otherwise the water flow can be restricted. The recommended diameters for maximum flow are:

13mm = 253 gph (gallons per hour) / 1,150 lph (litres per hour)
19mm = 506 gph / 2,300 lph
25mm = 792 gph / 3,600 lph
32mm = 1,495 gph / 6,800 lph
38mm = 2,991 gph / 13,600 lph

ABOVE **A useful design tip is to bend the line of stepping stones**

Supporting the stones within the pond is not always easy, but the stones must always end up perfectly stable and level, with no chance of them toppling over. This means that each must have a plinth or column virtually the same size as the stepping stone, allowing for only a minimal overhang. Each column has to be built up from the floor of the pond and end at a point where the stepping stone appears to float on the surface of the water.

Building onto the floor of a concrete pond is easy. A vertical column of bricks, blocks or stone can be simply built up – using mortar – to the required height.

Ponds made from flexible liners are a little more tricky. It is not ideal to place mortar directly onto the single layer of the base liner as pool liners may be damaged if the ground underneath has not been suitably prepared. Therefore a further protective film – perhaps thick PVC – should be placed on top of the liner before the column is built up on a thick bed of soft sand mortar.

Pre-moulded pools may have been installed with air gaps underneath – sometimes this is unavoidable. If a heavy weight, such as a stepping stone pillar, is applied directly over these, the plastic could buckle and split. It can, therefore, be risky placing columns in these sorts of pools.

Pieces of natural stone fit well into natural or informal ponds, and are available in all sorts of shapes and sizes, but they may eventually become rather slippery and, therefore, hazardous. There are obviously plenty of manufactured slabs to choose from – square, round, rectangular, hexagonal – but they are all of a limited size.

Timber decking squares can be used, but not if they have been treated with any toxic substances, which might wash off into the water. Hardwoods, cedar or any other naturally resilient timbers are more suitable than pressure-treated softwoods.

'BEACHES'

A sandy, muddy or stony 'beach', along one edge of a largish pond, can be eye-catching – it will set the scene for a completely different range of plants, and be a wonderful attraction for wildlife. Boulders, pebbles and even shells can be introduced to give the effect of the foreshore. If you desire it, an adjacent part of the garden could be given over to shingle, where an upturned boat could be at permanent rest, and deck chairs placed for looking at and sitting on – even the garden shed could be converted to look like a beach hut!

It is quite possible that the beach will occupy at least as much space as the pond itself. If a liner is used, it will mean extending it 3ft (1m) or more in one particular direction – don't be tempted to create the beach all the way around the pond: this would take up a huge amount of space and look ugly.

ABOVE **This gravel 'beach' will enable pond creatures to enter and exit the water safely**

ABOVE **A sand area for children can be separated from the water by decorative decking**

Excavation of the beach area should begin at its farthest point from the pond, with a vertical cut going down to about 9in (25cm). It can then slope very slightly down towards the main area of the pool before finally going down at about 45° into the deepest part of the pond. The laying of the liner is the same as for laying an ordinary pond (see page 24).

The only negative thing about a homemade freshwater beach, is that algae might grow in the shallow water – something which rarely happens in constantly washed seawater pools. However, most algae can be controlled by using an algacide from time to time.

MUDDY BEACHES

For one of these you will first need to build a fairly solid 6in (15cm) high retaining wall of old turves. Site this about 8in (20cm) back from the beginning of the 45° slope. To help keep the wall of turves in position, the bottom turf should

be much longer – perhaps 3ft (1m) – and draped over the edge, down into the deeper part of the pond. You then need to fill the area between the vertical part of the liner at the far end and the turf wall with a heavy clay loam (available as loam compost and sold in bags). Once the soil is in place, compact it and rake it so that the far end is at the same level as the adjacent garden soil or lawn. Next, slope the compacted soil gradually downwards until it meets the top of the turf wall; then, when the pond is filled, the water level will rise above the turf wall and be absorbed into the compacted soil to form the mud beach.

SANDY BEACHES

Similar to the mud beach, but this one can expand beyond the vertical section of liner. The sand within it will be wet, becoming progressively dry towards the furthest distance from the pond, whilst the sand outside of the liner will be as damp as the surrounding soil, or bone dry on a hot summer's day. Instead of a turf wall, the retaining wall for a sandy beach should be made from stone, mortared to hold it in place.

The types of planting used are important. Ornamental grasses, with spiky phormiums, yuccas and cordylines forming the backdrop, would be wholly appropriate.

JAPANESE-THEMED WATER FEATURES

Another option is a water garden with a wider theme – something in the style of a country, such as Japan, is the most popular.

A Japanese influence can bring an exotic and often sub-tropical feel to the garden, although the preconceived image of a Japanese garden rarely equates with that of the traditional art form. With such diverse cultures it is difficult to appreciate all aspects of each other's artistic creations, and a garden which adheres in every way to the influence of the Orient is unlikely to satisfy all the requirements of a modern western family.

However, the Japanese 'feel' can be achieved by planting, by the use of oriental materials like bamboo, by recreating some of the fundamental principles of Japanese landscape design and, of course, by appropriate use of water. In any Japanese-style garden water is central to the scheme, whether it be in the form of an elegantly shaped extensive pool, or as a simple bamboo shishi-odoshi (deer scarer), periodically spilling water into a bowl.

The shape of a 'Japanese' pool does not matter too much – as long as it is neither perfectly square nor round – for Japanese gardening is about creating a picture that brings the landscape of the countryside into the garden in a much reduced form. Islands can figure prominently, or the garden may feature mountainous representations, which are generally large rocks generously planted or closely associated with shrubby evergreens like the Japanese azalea or maple.

The oriental garden also uses the shoreline creatively. Rocks and planting create niches and promontories and, where water enters a pool from a stream, planting must conceal the entry.

A low, flat island alludes to a moor, and is usually planted with grasses, sedges and irises, while tidal islands are represented by almost completely submerged rocks interspersed with a tiny grassy planting.

Running water also figures strongly, and it is not confined to wandering streams, rills and cascades – it is even found in bamboo pipework. Large stones and coloured gravels that complement and contrast with each other can be used beneath water level along the pool edge.

Of the greatest importance, however, is the choice and arrangement of plants: not all need be from the Orient, but they must look right. Choose bamboos, grasses, irises, primulas and ferns. Where water is the focal point it is fun, and wholly appropriate, to grow a lotus.

ABOVE **Japanese-style bamboo features, like this shishi-odoshi, are becoming very popular**

ABOVE **Old water pumps will need a modern electric pump to work**

PUMPS

Let's face it, if you want something other than a still pond, then you are going to have to invest in a pump – unless you are lucky enough to have a natural stream or waterfall in your garden. There are essentially three types of water pump (other than the combined pump and filter sets covered in Chapter 4). The first, and most common, is the submersible pump, which sits within the body of water in the pond; this is attached to a hosepipe, which carries the circulated water up and away.

The second type of pump is designed to be used out of the water: the surface-only pump that is intended for use on dry land. It has the advantage of being extremely powerful, so water can be pumped over large distances, or very high for a spectacular display. It should be housed in a dry, well-ventilated area like a garage or shed, so as to avoid the problems that are associated with mixing electricity with water

(although there are in fact diesel- and petrol-powered versions). Because surface-only pumps are not under water, they can be stripped down and repaired more readily. These pumps are, however, expensive. They do not come with many of the 'extras', such as connectors, strainers, hoses and so on, which will be necessary components to the finished system, and all add to the cost.

The third and final type is the dual-purpose pump system, which can be used as a submersible pump or a surface pump. Some makes need to be housed at a lower level than the water level, so a separate tank is required. However, these pumps offer the flexibility for you to change your mind about their siting and use.

If you want to operate features like a waterfall and fountain independently, fitting one pump for each feature might prove more satisfactory.

The performance of any pump is affected by the following variables: water temperature, pipe width and length, any angles in the pipework or connectors and the number of water features. With specific features there are such factors as the intended heights of fountains and falls, and the volume of water. All of these can bring about friction loss which will affect your vertical head, that is, the maximum height to which the pump can deliver water. For all of these reasons, it is generally advisable to buy a pump that slightly exceeds the maximum amount of flow that your feature(s) will need.

To calculate the right size of pump for your pond, you need to ascertain the volume of water. For a circular pool, measure from the centre to the side and square it, then multiply the result by 3.14. Multiply this by the depth of the pool (in feet) and multiply the result by 6.25 for the volume in gallons.

LEFT **A typical modern submersible pump will enable the pond-keeper to run a fountain or waterfall**

ABOVE **Lighting will transform a pond or patio area at night**

Take a minute to digest this and try to work it out for yourself – you don't need to be Einstein! If you want to know the volume of your pond in litres it is easiest to convert the total gallonage directly, by referring to a conversion chart. Please note that one gallon equals 4.546 litres.

You will need a pump that can circulate a volume equivalent to the total volume in your pond every two hours. All good pumps will declare on the packaging the quantity of water they will move, so this is not a difficult decision. What is difficult, however, is choosing from the dozens of makes and models available.

LIGHTING

This can work its magic and bring water alive at night. Interesting effects can be created by using coloured lights to illuminate water descending down a waterfall or cascade, or on the upward and downward flow of a fountain. Witness some of our grand public fountains in city centres for spectacular night-time displays.

This may sound like something only a technical expert would attempt. Not so. Modestly priced kits are available from most garden centres, and with them often come different coloured lights. Sophisticated versions even change colours with moving discs travelling across the bulbs.

Lighting installation requires a degree of care and attention, as with all outdoors appliances. Low-voltage lighting is particularly easy and quick to install, with simple push-fit connections. You can even combine in-pond lights with garden lighting on the same cable.

RIGHT **Pond lights can be completely submerged. They come in a range of styles, some with coloured lenses**

CHAPTER 4

Clean water

The most discouraging factor for novice pond-keepers is the murkiness or greenness of the water. It is, therefore, useful to have an appreciation of the science of water, even if you don't understand it completely.

Essentially, 'green' water is the effect produced by millions of microscopic plants – actually algal cells – in suspension. This type of algae is invariably caused by an imbalance of pond-water nutrients, and the culprits are usually fish. These produce both ammonia and phosphate as waste which, as every keen gardener knows, make excellent fertilizers. Introducing aquatic plants and oxygenators into the water while it is green would be a waste, because algae prevent light from reaching the plants, so their growth is restricted.

LIFE CYCLE OF A POND

CLEAN WATER
either as fresh mains water when the pond is filled, or as on-going 'clear' water

USED WATER
caused by soil, run-off from surrounding ground, fish waste and excess, i.e. uneaten fish food

DISEASED WATER
if water is not treated heterotrophic bacteria, which carry diseases, settle in the water

RAIN & WATER
rain from the atmosphere fills our ponds and tops up our mains supplies

EXCESS
nitrates and phosphates not able to be absorbed by plants will lead to problems – methane gas, blanketweed, algae, acid water, lack of oxygen at night, etc

AMMONIA
this will be created in severe instances

OXYGEN & NITROGEN
water plants repay us by returning these two elements to the atmosphere

PLANT FOODS
nitrates – not nitrites – and phosphates are all good to have, in small quantities, in all ponds, for consumption by aquatic plants

NITRIFYING BACTERIA
nitrites are broken down by nitrifying bacteria

NITRITE
and if the water is not treated once ammonia is created, nitrite will be formed. This is particularly deadly to fish

ABOVE **Green water is caused by high levels of algae**

So, if you are going to invest in a pond, it will pay to have a reasonably clear understanding of the life cycle of the water before you begin.

It starts off clean, then gets polluted with fish waste and soil. These cause ammonia and various other toxicities, which mostly turn into nitrites; these then get broken down into plant foods (which is good), and the excess causes blanketweed, algae, acidic water and oxygen starvation (which is bad).

The accompanying flow-chart will help to put this life cycle into context, but the underlying message is that the water in your pond needs to be healthy.

TESTING

As the slightest change to the water chemistry of your pond can have a major effect on the life in it, it is advisable to test the water, and there are a number of kits available that will check levels of pH, ammonia, nitrate, nitrite and protein for you quickly and easily. However, with such a wide choice available, deciding which kit to buy is a bit like buying vitamins – do you opt for one to deal with

specific needs in mind or do you try an all-round multi-vitamin for optimum health? Fortunately there are several kits which include tests for all the following.

pH LEVELS

pH is the measure of acidity or alkalinity of a substance and high levels will affect the health of your fish and plants. Acidic water is lower than pH6.5, whereas alkaline water is higher than pH7.5. The figure of pH7 and a little either side of it are referred to as being 'neutral'. Most pond fish require a level between pH6.5 and pH7.5. Levels over pH8.5 can restrict plant growth as well as cause stress to your fish, which can in turn lead to infection and disease.

AMMONIA

Even the lowest levels of ammonia will stress fish, making them susceptible to infection and disease, so any sign of ammonia should be treated as an emergency situation for fish. High levels of ammonia in pond water are usually caused by over-stocking of fish, or too much detritus (uneaten food, fish waste, decaying plants and even dead insects).

NITRITE AND NITRATE

If ammonia in the pond is not treated, nitrites and nitrates will form. The former are highly toxic and very dangerous to fish, whilst the latter are non-toxic, and high levels act as plant nutrients, which leads to the growth of algae.

PROTEIN

The build-up of animal proteins in the water is usually due to the remains of food, fish waste and decomposing organisms. If untreated, these will lead to higher pH levels, a build-up of ammonia, nitrites and nitrates. If the results of your tests have highlighted any areas for improvement, then it is essential to take action as soon as possible.

TREATMENT

Some general treatments are made from evaporated seawater. These can temporarily block the toxic effects of nitrite in the water and replace electrolytes such as potassium, sodium, chloride, calcium and magnesium, which are all essential for the uptake of oxygen and the release of carbon dioxide and ammonium, which fish lose in times of stress.

There are also treatments that can be used for aesthetic problems such as unsightly sludge, algae or surface foam. In most cases these will come in the form of sachets of dry granules which are sprinkled over the pond. Be careful not to exceed the dosage.

The chemical treatments for clearing cloudy water – generally caused by suspended algae – work by bonding some of the suspended particles. This makes them heavy enough to either fall to the bottom of the pond, or to be removed by filtration.

Finally, if you need to place your fish in fresh tap-water, there are treatments to neutralize the water and make it safe for them.

POND FILTRATION AND UV CLARIFIERS

Why bother with a filtration system in your pond? After all, natural ponds and larger still waters don't have artificial filters, and they can generally support fish quite happily. Well, it's not quite as simple as that: a good filter is the only way to keep water crystal clear, while at the same time keep fish in tip-top condition.

The wild fish in our rivers and lakes don't always get it their own way, of course. They are at the behest of the elements, natural predators and anglers. However, in one important respect, they have a major advantage over their domesticated pond-dwelling cousins – they can swim off to pastures new if the water quality around them deteriorates. Garden ponds are quite limited environments when contrasted with the natural vastness of rivers and lakes, and pond fish are completely at our mercy.

Clear water is not necessarily clean water. Having the bottom of a 3ft (1m) pond in clear, visible focus is very much a priority for us but fish don't generally care what they can or cannot see. For example, sight plays a tiny part in the life of our wild carp, which spend virtually all their lives stirring up the sediment into an impenetrable cloud in their search for food!

ABOVE **Clear water is essential if you are trying to replicate something like a mountain stream**

POND FACT

With UV lamp wattages, a safe ratio is ten watts per 1,000 gal (4,546 litres). But, if your pond is very shallow, contains few plants with surface-shading leaves, or is exposed to full sunlight for most of the day, then it's a good idea to go for a lamp that is up a size from that recommended for your pond volume.

HOW FILTERS WORK

There are three basic methods of filtration: chemical, mechanical and biological. Each has a part to play, in varying degrees of importance.

Chemical filtration

Here, the filter medium exerts a chemical influence on the water as it passes through. We can generally discount this as a long-term filtration option, although there are times when it is useful. For example, zeolite is a chemical filter medium and is capable of absorbing ammonia from the water. It comes in the form of light grey or light brown chippings, made from hydrated silicates of calcium and aluminium (and sometimes with sodium and potassium).

Chemical filtration really comes into its own when a pond and filter are first set up, and the chemical and nitrogenous balance in the water has not been stabilized; in other words, the system is going through the process of maturation.

Mechanical filtration

This is the mechanical removal of solid waste as the water passes through a suitable medium such as foam, synthetic fibre or even gravel. The trapped solids are periodically removed from the system by hand. The filter can then be flushed through with clean water, under a tap.

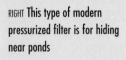

RIGHT **This type of modern pressurized filter is for hiding near ponds**

Many modern mechanical filters have an in-built ultra violet (UV) clarifier, and they work together to give clear water. A UV clarifier is not a filter in itself, but it makes algae clump together and they then strain out easily as the water they are floating in passes through the filter. Removal of solids also means that the most important aspect of filtration – the biological stage – works efficiently.

Biological filtration

This method makes use of natural biological processes to purify the water. It is also, arguably, the most important element in keeping fish alive. Although they vary in design, all biological filters support a colony of aerobic bacteria (i.e. those that flourish in oxygen-rich conditions) which convert toxic ammonia into progressively less harmful substances that are then recycled. This is the so-called 'nitrogen cycle'. The biological filtration process is as follows:

1 During decomposition, fish waste and other organic debris is converted to ammonia compounds by bacteria and fungi in the pond. These can be injurious to the fish.

2 A biological filter will begin its work by trapping larger dirt particles in the first layer of foam (this is purely 'mechanical').

3 Nitrosomonas bacteria, contained within the biological filter, then consume the harmful ammonia compounds and convert them to nitrites.

4 Unfortunately, the nitrites are just as toxic to the fish as the ammonia. Again, the filter comes into play with a population of Nitrobacter bacteria that convert the nitrites to nitrates. The nitrates do not affect the fish but fertilize the pond plants and algae.

5 The cycle is completed, because the pond fish eat the plants and algae.

POND FACT

It is pure folly to consider keeping koi in a pond without a filter. The waste from one of these fish over 14in (35cm) in length dramatically increases. A number of them would put a huge demand on any filtration system, so with no system at all the chance of keeping even small specimens is slim and a waste of money.

A large planted pond with few fish is indeed viable without a filter, but the 'safe' stocking rate for fish is 20–30in (50–75cm) length of fish per 1,000 gal (4,546 litres). At this rate you would be lucky to spot the fish between the plants, unless it was feeding time or they were basking in the sun. A fountain, which increases the oxygen level in the water, would mean that the pond was capable of supporting a greater head of fish, but in nothing like the numbers made possible by even the simplest filtration package.

FILTER DESIGNS

There is a wide choice of filters available, catering for everyone, from the beginner with a small pond, to the specialist with a large pool full of valuable fish.

The main problem with smaller pump-fed filters is that they are not adequately equipped to deal with the solids loading – they fall down mechanically, requiring such frequent maintenance that pond-keeping ceases to be a pleasure. If you can afford it, and have room for it, opt for a filter that is larger than the minimum recommended for your size of pond. The larger the filter, then the longer the intervals will be between cleanings.

A major drawback with the larger filters, however, is that they are usually highly visible. Downflow models have to be installed fully above the ground, and upflow versions can be only partially buried. If they are installed at the top of a waterfall it is quite easy to conceal them, but then the greater 'head' (the distance between pond surface and filter outflow point) will reduce pumping capacity.

A pump-fed, pressurized filter with integral UV clarifier is the answer. This can be sited anywhere around the pond – topping a cascade, buried in the adjoining ground to lid level or simply stood on a level base. Because water exits under pressure it can be piped up to a waterfall header pool, or simply returned via a hose to the pond.

Pressurized filters actually force dirty water through the foam media rather than relying on gravity, and so many more solids can be trapped before the foam needs a clean. The UV lamp is contained within the pressurized canister and all water has to pass by it on its way back to the pond.

FILTER PUMPS

The pump that drives a filter must be of the solids-handling type, quite different from the one used to power a fountain. Fountain pumps do incorporate a strainer, but this is partly so their impellers are not clogged and partly to prevent dirt particles travelling up to the fountain nozzle and blocking the jet. Solids-handling pumps are designed to take all the debris out of the pond and into the filter.

OXYGENATING PLANTS

There is only one real reason to have pondweeds, or oxygenating plants, in your pond, and that is to provide oxygen, which in turn helps to keep the water stable and in good condition. Of all the plants we can add to our ponds, these are perhaps the least interesting, yet they are almost certainly the most important.

If there are too many fish, or not enough plants (particularly the oxygenating type) in your pond, then the water becomes short of dissolved oxygen.

This manifests itself in fish either gasping for air at the surface, or lurking at the bottom, utterly disinterested in their food. If you add outside influences such as lack of water movement and a spell of still, sultry weather that warms up the water so it can hold even less dissolved oxygen, you can very readily end up with some extremely sick fish.

Increasing the oxygen level in the water is not difficult. You can turn on the fountain or waterfall (if you have one), which will add and mix oxygen into the water as it tumbles and turns. However, if you have a still pond, the simplest thing to do is to make sure you have a plentiful and permanent supply of cheap and easy-to-grow oxygenating plants.

These are usually green, they rarely flower and seem to spend their lives suspended in the water, growing rapidly when your back is turned and never when you want them to. By day they convert dissolved carbon dioxide, given off by the fish, into oxygen. They also consume minerals and nutrients that otherwise would be used by opportunist and troublesome algae.

A good selection of oxygenating plants will also provide effective cover for all manner of water creatures; fish will be afforded some protection against marauding herons, and spawning grounds will be provided for fish, amphibious and insectivorous wildlife.

Most garden centres will offer oxygenating plants from outside tanks and they are usually sold as small bunches of stems linked by a heavy metal weight. You just have to drop these bunches into the pond – you don't need planting baskets or compost. The weights will take the bases of the bunches down, and they will find their own level, depending on the amount of leaves, and start to grow.

Most oxygenators will grow rapidly, especially during warm summers, and can cause the pond to become congested. Therefore it is important to hook out a few buckets' worth of excess weed, perhaps two or three times during the summer period. This will, curiously, make the weed grow faster, and this in turn makes it more efficient at filtering and conditioning the water.

ABOVE **Canadian pondweed (*Elodea canadensis*) is an excellent oxygenator but needs to be controlled**

Carefully check through the foliage as you're removing it, spread it out by the side of the pond and leave it for a day so that any creatures caught up in it, and which can crawl back into the water, are given the best chance.

Add the semi-dried weed to the compost heap. On no account be inclined to take it to your local pond or stream to keep it alive. Many misguided aquarists and pond owners have done this in the past, thus introducing plants that have quickly crowded out our native pond plant species and upsetting the whole ecology of our natural waterways.

It's a good idea to select several species of oxygenator so that a variety of wildlife will be attracted. All wild pond-inhabiting creatures have their particular likes and dislikes, and a variety of foliage shapes and growth habits will offer the most habitats. Some of the best oxygenators include:

ABOVE **Water milfoil** (*Myriophyllum aquaticum*)

> **POND FACT**
> Topping up a pond with rainwater from a butt discourages blanketweed.

Callitriche hermaphroditica (Autumn starwort)
A delicate plant, with vivid green foliage and fragile stems, that grows all year. It is prone to damage by heavy-finned fish.

Elodea canadensis (Canadian pondweed)
Probably the most commonly seen oxygenator, it is hardy, vigorous and ideal for new ponds.

Potamogeton crispus (Curled pondweed)
The long, crinkled leaves can be slow to establish, but are very sturdy, making the plant good for ponds with waterfalls or fountains.

Ceratophyllum demersum (Hornwort)
This free-floating plant has dark green, feathery foliage, and may need securing by tying to a stone or weight.

Myriophyllum aquaticum (Water milfoil)
There are about 40 different water milfoils worldwide, all making superb perennial oxygenating plants with attractive blue-green or brown fern-like leaves in artistic whorls. But there are only a small handful that are regularly found in our domestic outdoor ponds. *Myriophyllum aquaticum* is the most commonly seen, with very dense ferny foliage that emerges stiffly from the water. It is a tropical species and tends to die back in winter to dormant crowns that rest well beneath the surface of the water. These crowns then re-emerge in spring.

Hottonia palustris (Water violet)
This floating plant also produces flowers and has immense ornamental value (see page 98).

GENERAL MAINTENANCE

Finally, there are a number of mechanical aids which help us keep our ponds clean and therefore clear:

NETS

Removing floating debris is fairly straightforward – an ordinary pond net will often do the trick, although it needs time and patience if you are chasing small bits of debris around the pond surface.

POND VACUUMS

For most of us, the thought of 'cleaning out the pond' fills us with horror because it's a slippery and smelly job. Removing debris and sludge from the bottom of the pond can be fairly difficult, though we are fortunate these days to have aquatic vacuum cleaners to help us out. Remember, however, that a pond vacuum will not turn a cloudy pond into a crystal clear lagoon. It removes the silt, sludge, detritus and potentially toxic substances from the bottom of the pond. Hence algal growth is largely reduced, the water becomes clearer over a period of time, and filter systems are made more efficient. A side benefit is that garden beds and borders will be treated to a fine watery manure which they'll lap up (especially on hungry or chalky soils).

Most pond vacuum sets comprise a collecting tank with motor unit and over 30ft (10m) of cable, a 16ft (5m) suction hose, an 8ft (2.5m) discharge hose, a hose-end connector, extension tubes and adjustable suction nozzles.

ABOVE **Use a pond vacuum to remove silt and sludge from the pond**

Some more sophisticated types even include a radio remote control with battery and holder.

Operating these pond vacuums is not difficult. The unit should always be at least 6ft (2m) away from the pond edge. Place the end of the discharge hose where the muddy water is to be released when the collecting tank is emptied. This effluent can be directed over any bed, ideally between plants to hide any discoloration of the soil. Connect the unit to the power supply via an RCD and switch it on.

Guide the nozzle to the bottom of the pond, and move it slowly and evenly to vacuum up the mud. When the collecting tank has been filled to its maximum level, a float valve automatically switches off the vacuuming operation, indicated by a high-pitched motor noise. At this point, take the nozzle out of the water and tilt the hose up to allow the remaining water to drain into the tank. Then switch off the unit.

POND SCISSORS

These are supplied with handles around 45in (115cm) long and are very helpful for cutting through dead weeds; they are particularly effective for the dreaded blanketweed, which can smother plants and choke fish.

POND FACT

When planting a new pond, aim to add five to seven stems of oxygenating plants for every 2sq ft (0.18m²) of surface area.

CHAPTER 5

Hardy pond fish

Much of the enjoyment derived from a pond is as a result of the fish that swim around in it. In fact I feel that a pond is not complete if it doesn't have some fish, which add colour and animation to the scene, particularly in formal pools. A side benefit is that they can reduce significantly the number of midges and mosquitoes that frequent your garden. It is, however, important to understand that fish can vary greatly in their requirements, so much so that a pond which is perfect for one species, may be a deathtrap for another. For this reason I am going to explain which fish do what, and how to make your pond the best environment for them.

BUYING POND FISH

Once you have built your pond and filled it with tap-water, the urge to put some fish in it can be enormous. Don't. A new pond must settle down – six weeks is not an unrealistic time to wait – before introducing fish. During the first couple of weeks the fresh water in the pond will turn a browny-green colour, and become progressively cloudier as micro-organisms multiply. A variety of plants should be in place, including plenty of submerged oxygenators. These will help to absorb dissolved minerals, and of course provide oxygen to the water. The fish will be afforded some protection by these, and will also use them for green food. Floating and deep-water plants provide the shade which is very welcome on hot summer days. By the sixth week the water should be clear.

It is worth remembering that most fish scavenge. They'll nose around and disturb freshly planted aquatics, so it is important to allow the plants time to establish before the fish are introduced, and to cover the soil in the pots with a thick layer of gravel, otherwise the soil will be displaced, and the water will turn brown.

Buying some fish from a garden centre, transporting them home, and then putting them

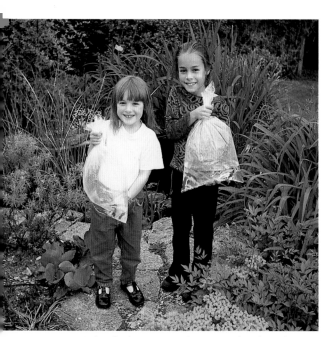

ABOVE Fish make decorative – and comparatively undemanding – pets for children

in the pond, with no forethought about the environment they were in, and the one to which you are now subjecting them, can result in a high, if not total, mortality rate. So, to start with, it is essential to know just how many fish, and of what size, your pond can accommodate safely. Work this out before you start spending money on buying the fish (see box on page 58). Of course, you may exceed the recommended quantity of fish under certain conditions if, for instance, you have a pond that is very deep, or you have installed an over-sized filtration system, but this is unlikely for a beginner to the hobby.

The best time to stock a new pond, or add further fish to an existing complement, is in late spring or early summer when temperatures are fairly stable but when buying fish you do take a bit of a gamble. No one can say with 100% conviction whether a fish is absolutely free of disease or parasites, regardless of how healthy it may look. This six-point plan for detecting signs of a healthy fish should serve as a useful guide.

1 Look for a lively disposition. Fish such as goldfish, orfe and koi should be constantly on the move, and even dart about when 'spooked'. If they seem lethargic, or float on the surface, or lie relatively still at the bottom, then they are best avoided. However, note that bottom-dwellers, like tench, should be at the bottom and they move quite slowly – this is normal.

2 Check the fins. A healthy fish should have its fins well extended. The fin on the back (the dorsal) regularly extends and collapses as the fish hovers or changes direction; it is usually collapsed as the fish moves its tail fin (the caudal) to propel itself forward. Any damaged fins will indicate that the fish has been in a scrap, and it should be avoided.

3 Look at the body. Damaged or missing scales are unsightly, but not necessarily a sign of ill health. Scales can usually regenerate without subsequent infection. However, if there any

blood spots, or fungal growth (looking like cotton wool), then do not buy it – or other fish from the same tank.

4 Examine the eyes. A healthy fish should have clear eyes. If they are 'milky' in appearance, it is a possible sign that the fish is injured or otherwise unhealthy. This can be difficult if the fish you want is moving about quickly, or hugging the bottom of the tank, but it is worth taking the time to find out.

5 Check the colours. The scales of a fish are covered by a protective layer of mucus, which tends to enhance the colour of the fish and make the body bright, vivid and clear. If the fish is unhealthy, there can be a check to the mucus, or an excess in the production of mucus, both of which can cause the appearance to be dull or cloudy.

6 Observe the swimming technique. A regular pace, in straight lines, and in a considered way. This is how a healthy fish should swim. It should not roll about, or lose its balance, or keep floating upwards, or sinking downwards. The one word of caution here is if a fish is eating, or has just had a meal, it can sometimes sway as it chews.

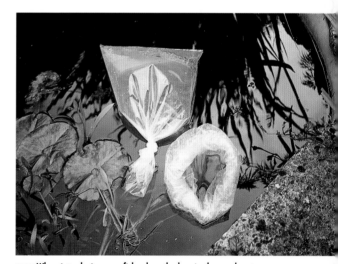

ABOVE **When introducing new fish, place the bag in the pond water for about ten minutes**

POND FACT
When deciding how many fish can safely be introduced to your pond, follow this equation: allow 24sq in (155cm²) of water surface area per 1in (2.5cm) length of fish – excluding tails! Once the calculation has been made, reduce it by 25%, to allow for the fish to grow.

INTRODUCING FISH

Fish make great pets for children, but are highly sensitive to changes in temperature and water quality, so avoid any shocks when transferring them to the pond. When you buy fish from a pet shop or aquatic centre they will be swimming around in a plastic bag. After a trip in the car (and particularly if the fish were previously housed in an indoor aquarium), the water will be warm, or at least the equivalent of 'room temperature'. So, for best results, follow this simple process:

1 Place the bag containing the fish in the pond, and leave it for ten minutes so that the water temperature inside the bag reduces to the same as the pond water.

2 Introduce a little pond water into the bag. Leave for ten minutes.

ABOVE **Gradually allow some of the pond water into the bag**

3 Add a little more water and leave for a further ten minutes.

4 Push the bag on to its side so that the fish can swim away freely. Remember at all times that fish are living creatures, and if you treat them right they will reward you with life, vitality, colour and even friendliness. Get a routine in your feeding and as long as you don't frighten them, they'll start to trust you and come up to you.

SPECIES TO CHOOSE

There are in excess of 20,000 species of fish in nature, and most of these are marine-based. In comparison there is just a small number of freshwater fish and only a tiny proportion of these are suitable for keeping in ponds. Nevertheless, of the few species available to us, there is a huge range of hybrids, shapes, colours, habits and sizes. And the good news is that every few years a new type of fish, or strain of fish, becomes available to the pond-keeper.

THE COMMON GOLDFISH

Description: It is said that the common goldfish is the best-known fish in the world and we can all instantly recognize it. It is fairly long-lived fish – 15 years is not unusual – and millions are bred annually by fish farms, which also makes them quite cheap to buy.

Originally from China and parts of Siberia, the goldfish is a hardy breed, able to withstand a range of temperatures from above 86°F (30°C) down to practically freezing. As a child I well remember the cold British winter of 1963. We had about eight goldfish in a large metal water tank in the greenhouse. The water froze solid, even under glass, all bar about three inches at the bottom. They were probably iced up for three or four days in total but, by speedily defrosting the ice, we managed to save most of the fish.

Goldfish can grow up to about 12in (30cm) from head to tail, if the conditions are right and the pool large enough. Fancy varieties are usually considerably smaller. The 'normal' goldfish is short-finned, usually orange but also in other single colour variations (although curiously not in the olive green that is the natural colour of its ancestors).

Varieties: Centuries of selective breeding have produced over 100 'official' varieties of goldfish. Here are some of the most commonly seen:

Bristol shubunkin Shubunkins are fancy versions of the goldfish with larger fins and generally with more graceful, ornamental qualities. The Bristol is single-tailed, long-finned and has mottled coloration which normally includes a little blue.

Comet These are sleeker cousins of the shubunkin, with a longer tail, preferably pointed.

Moor Double-tailed black fish, sometimes with protruding eyes, rather more tender than the others. Today there are varieties with chocolate, and chocolate and orange colourings.

Ranchu Oval-bodied, with a curved back profile minus the dorsal fin. Usually orange.

Veiltail. Oval-bodied and double-tailed, with long, flowing fins.

Fancies Fantails and Orandas are tender and are really at their best in a coldwater aquarium.

POND FACT

When fish are prone to disease, sudden death and red fins, this is a sure sign that the water has a high level of acidity (or low pH). Other indications are when oxygenating plants do not multiply well; biological pond filters do not work properly and water snails develop thin, pitted shells.

When fish are prone to fungal diseases and gill disorders, this is a sure sign that the water has a high level of alkalinity (or high pH). Other indications are when oxygenating plants are covered in a slimy coating; water plants display a yellowing of the leaves when in full growth and the water smells slightly of ammonia.

However, they make good pond inhabitants for the warmer months.

Breeding: Most goldfish possess the same habits, i.e. they eat their own eggs! The mature females scatter the eggs amongst water plants, usually when the temperature rises above 68°F (20°C) – conditions can certainly be favourable in late spring, particularly in shallow waters.

ABOVE **Keeping pond fish can reduce significantly the number of midges and mosquitoes frequenting your garden**

GOLDEN ORFE

Description: Golden orfe, also known as the 'ide' fish, are perfect for larger ponds – with a minimum surface area of 43sq ft (4m²). In the wild the orfe is silver, but the golden form has been bred for use in garden ponds, along with blue and marbled variants. They are native to various parts of northern Europe, particularly the River Danube. They are fast movers, staying near the surface of the water – a very obliging form of behaviour as far as humans are concerned.

Orfe are usually sold as specimens of 3–4in (8–10cm) long, but in time they will reach 18in (45cm) if conditions are right. They need to swim in water that is oxygen rich and for this reason they seem to enjoy the splashes from fountains and waterfalls. They can suffer when the oxygen runs low, for instance during dull, thundery weather.

Breeding: In late spring the female scatters her eggs among fine-leaved water plants. Hatching takes place in around 20 days.

GOLDEN TENCH

Description: This fish, which in the wild inhabits the still waters of rivers, large ponds and even sand pits, can grow to a massive 28in (71cm), although 12–16in (30–41cm) is more usual for a healthy adult in a large domestic pond. Tench are excellent scavengers and feed off the muddy bottoms of the pond. Although they are very hardy fish, during particularly cold weather they will bury themselves in the mud for some protection.

The original, if you like 'wild' form, was the green tench but for garden pond situations the cultivated golden tench is better, as it is more decorative and more easily seen.

Tench are undemanding, being able to survive in relatively acidic water (low pH), with fairly low oxygen levels. The natural food of the tench comprises various insects, worms and young shoots of water vegetation.

Breeding: a mature female can lay up to 900,000 adhesive eggs among aquatic plants and weed in late spring and early summer. Hatching can take between six and eight days.

GOLDEN RUDD

Description: The body of this fish is actually silver, but with a golden hue. Its scales are large and rough-looking, and make identification fairly easy. In a pond situation the rudd can grow to 16in (41cm) in length, feeding on worms, insects and certain aquatic vegetation. It is found wild in slow-running rivers in most parts of Europe north of the Pyrenees.

The rudd inhabits the surface and midwater section of the pond, and associates well with other fish, particularly orfe.

Breeding: a large female rudd can lay as many as 200,000 adhesive eggs during spring and early summer. Hatching takes between eight and 15 days, depending on the temperature.

GRASS CARP

Description: This species can grow to over 3ft (1m) in length so a large pond is required. Although it is a fine fish, with certain excellent qualities, I hesitate to recommend it: firstly, because it consumes large amounts of most water plants with relish; and secondly because the larger fish can also leap, so it is not unusual for them to jump out of the pond and perish. In its favour, most grass carp kept in ornamental pools are albinos, which are particularly attractive against dark-sided ponds, and they will actually consume quantities of unwanted vegetation, including duckweed and algae.

Breeding: this fish needs a temperature of around 80–84°F (27–29°C) to spawn, so is unlikely to breed in the confined ponds of temperate zone gardens (which, bearing in mind their eventual size, is quite possibly a relief to know).

FEEDING FISH

Providing clean water and supplying the correct, balanced food, are the two most important considerations for fish.

Fish are generally omnivorous, naturally eating both plant and animal material, some species scouring the bottom of the pond for worms, shrimps, algae and even decaying detritus. So, if fish can survive without help in the wild, do our pond fish actually need any supplementary food from us? If you possess a lush wildlife pond teeming with insects and crustaceans, and have only a few fish, then the answer would be 'no'. But in most cases, providing supplementary food is the safest option for maintaining a healthy stock of fish.

Do not feed your fish at all if the temperature drops below 44°F (7°C). It is harmful to feed fish when it is so cold that their metabolic processes, slow right down, increasing the danger of food rotting inside the gut. Between 44 and 57°F (7–14°C), easily digestible foods with high wheatgerm content can be introduced. When the water temperature stabilizes above 59°F (15°C), use high protein, growth-inducing feed; increase the frequency of meals to two or three times a day as the temperature rises.

Skim off any remaining food from the surface if it has been uneaten after ten minutes or so. Failing to do this will result in surplus food falling to the bottom to be fed on by bacteria, whose toxic by-products can poison fish.

The main types of pond fish food are manufactured flakes and pellets, frozen aquatic organisms and live food. When buying manufactured food, look out for types that float well, bringing the fish to the surface to feed. Choose a size that is appropriate to your fish. Like us, fish need a balanced diet, so check the packet to ensure that the protein content – fishmeal, soya and egg mainly – is around 30% for summer foods.

For spring and autumn feeding change to makes with proportionately higher carbohydrate (wheatgerm-based) levels. Vitamin C is also useful as it boosts fish immunity to disease, and is added to some higher-quality foods.

If you wish to adopt a more organic approach to feeding your fish, it is possible to buy many of the organisms that fish would encounter in the wild. Earthworms, chopped lettuce, the occasional slice of orange (peel and all) are all nutritious additions.

ABOVE **Look out for types of manufactured fish food that float well**

CHAPTER 6

Introduction to koi keeping

The fish with the best social mastery are the koi (real name nishikigoi). They will feed from your hand quite readily, and over a period of time they can be seen to develop characters of their own. But to keep even one koi successfully, you should provide relatively sophisticated filtration, water movement and oxygenation, year-round care, special food and, of course, regularly check and maintain high water quality. Keeping koi requires investment and dedication.

ABOVE **Koi are voracious eaters and can tear plants to pieces**

Although koi are descendants of the common carp their selective breeding over the years has meant that they are much more particular about the water conditions in which they live. Maintenance of good water quality all year round is, therefore, of the utmost importance.

Great pleasure is gained from viewing koi swimming lazily in clear, clean water, watching them grow and their patterns change as they develop and age. It is, therefore, the general rule that a koi pond will not be planted. Some people do keep koi alongside other coldwater fish, quite successfully, in planted 'ornamental' ponds. Keeping large koi in these conditions can, however, present problems. Because koi are voracious creatures that will tear plants to pieces, a planted pond is generally not feasible. Some parts of the plants will be eaten but others will sink to the bottom of the pond, whilst other pieces may be sucked into a submersible pump. Even if plants are not shredded by the koi, large-leafed plants such as lilies will act as perfect hiding places, preventing the koi from being seen easily.

Water depth – which aids body shape development – and volume in a koi pond are important considerations. After all, koi can grow to lengths above 2ft (60cm), and will do so in just a few years given the right conditions. Therefore, even a beginner's pond should be no less than say, 3,000gal (13.5m^3). Ideally, the depth of a koi pond should be 4ft 6in (1.35m) or more.

POND FACT
Keeping koi as a worldwide hobby – rather than as a home-grown one in Japan – only came about in the late 1960s, when transportation was made possible by the invention of the polythene bag.

BUYING KOI

Most newcomers to the koi-keeping hobby are eager to improve their stock. Consequently they spend, or should spend, many happy hours in the company of fellow hobbyists, or with dealers, discussing, selecting and, ultimately, purchasing. This latter element can be expensive, particularly if the fish are brought home to inadequate facilities and perish – often in a surprisingly short period of time. The new keeper will have learnt a salutary lesson in that the correct facilities, including an adequate filter, must be in place before buying.

It is best to purchase one, or at the most two fish at a time, preferably separated by at least a couple of weeks to allow the filter system to adjust to the additional load. Daily water testing is the norm at these times (see 'Avoiding koi stress' on pages 66–67).

The quality of a koi is judged by factors such as skin quality, body shape, pattern and depth of coloration and the fish exhibiting the best of these desirable characteristics are currently bred in Japan. However, Japan is not the only producer of koi, and these days stocks from countries such as Israel, Singapore, Korea, Thailand, the USA and the UK are improving all the time.

If the pond-keeper wants to increase or improve koi stock, the country of origin should be taken into account as some places are very warm, with little or no winter. A koi's metabolism approaches its most efficient point at temperatures above 20°C (70°F). It follows, therefore, that during the winter – when the water temperature drops below 10°C (50°F) – the immune systems of our koi are not at their best for repelling the various pathogens that abound in our ponds. Furthermore, variable spring and autumn temperatures can cause overnight swings of 5°C (40°F) or more in small volumes of water. This can affect the koi, causing them to be stressed and maybe to succumb to disease or illness.

This fact alone can cause losses in koi ponds, particularly in springtime when the digestive systems of the fish stop and start on a regular basis. This is why a koi-keeping hobby is an all-year-round one requiring vigilance at all times.

POND FACT
Koi are poikilothermic – meaning that their body temperature takes up that of their surroundings. During the winter their body temperature falls along with the air and water temperature.

IDENTIFICATION
Because Japan is the home of the koi, and this is where much of the breeding has taken place, koi are regularly referred to globally by their Japanese classes and variety names. The first thing to observe when trying to identify a class of koi is its scales. Does it have a metallic sheen? Metallic koi, because of their shiny, vivid coloration, really stand out in a pond, and are therefore often the first choice for beginners to the hobby. As koi-keeping skills are improved, then the more variable and arguably more interesting varieties are experimented with. These include the Go-Sanke varieties such as Tancho Sanke, Kohaku and Showa.

ABOVE **Most of these koi are Kohaku – red markings on a white base**

ABOVE **It is vitally important that koi are fed with specially formulated koi food**

POND FACT
The true name for koi is nishikigoi, which means 'brocaded carp'. The accepted contraction of nishikigoi is koi, but actually means 'carp'. Therefore, if you refer to koi as 'koi carp' you are actually calling them 'brocaded carp carp'.

There are three classes of metallic koi varieties, and nine classes of non-metallic, with a further class for Kinginrin (fish that have shiny scales of any body type). Each class contains varieties that are determined by variations of colour and pattern. The following is a simplified breakdown of the classification system (note that the distinction between one class and another can be blurred, and even experts are regularly baffled).

METALLIC
Hikarimono: single-coloured metallic koi often in gold, silver, yellow, orange, grey and platinum variations
Hikarimoyomono: metallic orange or yellow on white
Hikariutsurimono: metallic forms of Utsurimono and Showa Sanshoko koi (see page 66)

NON-METALLIC

Kohaku: red markings on a white base

Tancho Sanke: red and black markings on a white base

Showa Sanshoko: red and white markings on a black base

Bekko: black markings on a red, yellow or white base colour

Utsurimono: red, yellow or white markings on a black base colour

Asagi and Shusui: body blue or dark blue, with red/orange belly

Koromo: red markings overlaid with darker patterning, on a white base colour

Tancho: single red spot on the top of the head

Kawarimono: all other forms of non-metallic koi, including single colours

AVOIDING KOI STRESS

I cannot emphasize too highly the importance of a stress-free environment for koi. Many factors make fish stressed, and the following five-point plan will alert you to the most severe.

1 Waste pollutants: these should be low, i.e. the water should be chemically clean. To achieve this, a biological filter of adequate size for the volume of fish population in the pond must be installed. Using a water-testing kit to ensure that the effect of fish respiration and waste have not made the water toxic by increased ammonia or nitrite levels is also essential. Basic kits can test for ammonia, nitrite, nitrate and pH, but where koi-keeping is concerned, testing for oxygen and carbonate hardness is important as well.

2 Insufficient vitamins and minerals: supplement these by feeding with good-quality food, specially formulated for koi.

ABOVE Avoid subjecting koi to stress: one of the fundamentals of this is providing a good supply of oxygen

3 Lack of oxygen: koi need a good supply of oxygen. Water circulated via some form of water course helps aeration and will normally provide sufficient oxygen, but most koi-keepers incorporate a venturi (a tube with a constriction to reduce or control fluid flow) or, preferably, an air pump into their system to provide the copious amount of oxygen required.

4 Heavy metals such as lead, copper and zinc: levels of these should be low or, better still, completely absent, as they can restrict growth, prevent reproduction and cause death if allowed to persist and accumulate in the koi's body. If a water quality report (normally free from your mains water supplier) shows these levels to be high in your incoming mains tap water, then an input water filter designed to remove these metals is advisable.

5 Variable levels of temperature: temperature stability is a parameter of water quality often overlooked, but variable levels can seriously affect the lives of the fish. Koi-keepers often add some form of thermostatically controlled heating to their pond system to achieve stability of temperature, and swings can be minimized by creating and using during the winter months a removable cover made from an insulating material such as bubble plastic.

As mentioned in Chapter 4, to enjoy a pond at its best the water should be clear, but the water clarity alone does not guarantee good water – indeed 'green' water has the benefit of developing the colours of koi. However, if the water is not clear, then viewing of these beautiful fish is restricted.

CHAPTER 7

Wildlife

The wildlife that take up residence in and around your water garden can provide as much enjoyment and fascination as any other aspect of pond-keeping.

Amazingly, if you had the most barren of gardens, dug a hole in the ground and lined it, then filled it with water and left it there, within a couple of months it would be teeming with wildlife. Flying insects such as beetles and dragonflies would move in – even if the nearest breeding groups were over two miles

(three kilometres) away – and amphibian reptiles like frogs and toads would appear as if from nowhere. Miniscule creatures are often carried on the wind from one watery haven to another – so why shouldn't they land at yours?

So, if all this can happen naturally, why deliberately set out to attract wildlife to a pond? To answer this we must understand why it is so important to preserve our wildlife heritage. The natural habitats for aquatic and amphibious wildlife – woodland or moorland streams, natural springs, village ponds, marshlands, clean rivers and so on – are disappearing as a result of changing agricultural and industrial land uses, new roads and spreading towns. This is exacerbated by the gradual climatic changes, which have caused many waterways – ponds and streams predominantly – to dry up. Therefore, if wildlife habitats are disappearing, then so is the wildlife itself.

In fact, domestic ponds do not always attract wildlife: formal pools, for example, which have straight sides, perhaps few plants, and maybe gushing fountains, will be fairly inhospitable places for insects and delicate aquatic creatures. So, too, will ponds that are geared up for crystal clear water, perhaps with sophisticated filters and UV clarifiers which can, of course, neutralize tiny creatures as well as unwanted algae.

Inviting wildlife to your pond, by making it a welcome place to inhabit, is a positive contribution to the threat. So, what can you do?

ABOVE **Pond snails feed on decaying plant matter**

RICH DIVERSITY OF LIFE: THE GOODIES

The following are beneficial creatures, and are generally attracted to gardens by the presence of a pond.

DAMSELFLIES AND DRAGONFLIES.

These beautiful creatures are usually bright red or blue. The larvae live under the water (up to five years in the case of some dragonflies), feeding on small creatures passing by. They gradually climb out of the pond to eventually emerge as adults. Damselflies are slightly daintier versions of the dragonfly, but as you can get red and blue versions of both, identification by colour alone is not wise. Both insects are found naturally wherever there is a large body of water, but more usually in country areas rather than towns or cities.

FRESHWATER SNAILS

These will probably need to be introduced to your pond either by accident or design (they can be purchased from aquatic centres, or they may come in unwittingly with water plants).

POND FACT

In a perfectly balanced garden there should be a stable food chain of prey and predator. For example, destroying all of the greenfly will deprive ladybirds and bluetits of food. And a garden without any slugs at all is unlikely to have any frogs or toads (even if there is a pond). Low populations of most pests should be tolerated and will encourage wildlife.

HELP TO ENCOURAGE WILDLIFE

We have already considered making a 'beach' (see Chapter 3), which is as much for encouraging wildlife as it is a decorative feature. Consider the following for making your water garden attractive for wildlife:

Do

◆ have an area of rockery near to the pond which can offer sanctuary to amphibians, such as frogs, toads and newts.
◆ create a central island within the pond, as a haven for small birds and insects.
◆ grow lush bog-garden plants, with a good canopy of leaves, to give small creatures essential protection.
◆ create a deep part of the pond, at least 3ft (1m), which is too deep for certain predators, and where water temperatures are stable.

◆ allow dead and decaying wood to become a feature of your wildlife pond, because these can support many types of insect, as well as fungi, mosses and lichens.
◆ (perhaps the most important of all) create some sort of platform, or sitting area, where you can observe (and feed) the wildlife at close quarters. The more you appreciate wildlife, the more you are likely to want to attract it.

Don't

◆ have pools with steep sides, which make it difficult for animals to get out of the water.
◆ stock large populations of ornamental fish, which will eat small creatures and plants.
◆ in larger areas, where waterfowl are welcome, don't put the pond near to large trees which would interrupt the flight access of waterfowl.

There are many different species of snail, some of which are tiny. Generally, snails are excellent at keeping ponds clean, as they feed on decaying plant matter and algae. The great pond snail also feeds on dead fish, soft-bodied invertebrates and even tadpoles. The flat ram's horn snail is particularly welcome as it feeds on algae and pondweed.

FROGS

These are possibly our most welcome visitors, roaming the garden devouring slugs and other garden pests as they go. Sometimes heavy frog populations can 'bully' residential fish, but this does not often become a serious problem. Frogs usually have a smooth skin, varying in colour from deep olive green to a pale mustard yellow. Sometimes they have distinct brick red hues: these are usually old or sick frogs and the reddish colour is an indication of the stresses their metabolism is undergoing. Adults spend most of the summer living in moist, shaded vegetation, but never far from the water. Frogs hibernate, and the males tend to take a deep breath before they sink to the bottom of the pond to dwell in the mud for two or three months. The females will generally hide beneath piles of garden debris, to lie undisturbed over the winter period.

ABOVE **Frogs are one of the garden's most welcome visitors**

From late winter, the frogs will begin the familiar spawning rituals. Soon large glutinous clumps of eggs are seen, which turn into thousands upon thousands of agitated tadpoles within weeks. These feed on pond algae initially but, as they age, become carnivore and eat small pond-dwelling invertebrates. Sadly for some tadpoles – which are, of course, small pond-dwelling invertebrates themselves – they will find that they are indeed food for their siblings. In other words, tadpoles are cannibals.

TOADS

These are mainly night-time feeders; the most widely seen toads are the common and natterjack toads, which are usually larger, wartier and more 'rounded' than frogs. They are rarer than frogs, and can hibernate up to a mile away from the spawning pond, under piles of leaves, in holes in the soil, and in similar refuges. They will eat slugs, as well as caterpillars, beetles, woodlice and even ants. Toads arrive at the spawning pond in mid-spring and soon after, amongst the submerged weed, strings of eggs can be seen, wound around the plant stems. These eventually hatch as tadpoles, and the story from here is the same as for frogs.

NEWTS

Smooth, crested and palmate newts are very shy, secretive creatures but they are just as beneficial as frogs and toads in eating garden pests. It is not easy to identify between the newt species, as there are times of year when they can closely resemble one another. For example, smooth newts are the most common, and adult males can grow to 4½in (11cm) in length. They are dark brown and spotted, with a distinctive crest in the spring and summer, which can often confuse their appearance with crested newts. Palmate newts meanwhile are much smaller, but can be confused with smooth newts. The great crested newt (*Triturus cristatus*) is a protected species. Newts emerge from hibernation –

ABOVE **The common smooth newt**

ABOVE **The palmate newt**

ABOVE **The crested newt**

generally from under pondside vegetation or large, flat stones – around mid-spring. Within a month they are engaged in an elaborate aquatic courtship, whereby the male moves around the female, waving his tail to give her his 'scent'. Eggs are laid individually, usually in submerged foliage.

POND SKATERS

There are ten species of pond skater – some will quickly fly in and inhabit a new pond, whilst those without wings must be carried to their new

ABOVE **Pond skaters spread their weight over the water**

home on plants. These endearing insects are easily recognizable, because they 'walk' on the surface of the water, in order to spread their weight over as large an area as possible. They feed on dead and dying insects, and effectively 'clean up' the surface of the water for us, albeit on a minuscule scale.

WATER BOATMAN

This familiar bug – actually a type of fly – swims just beneath the surface of the water, using its legs and body like a boat being powered by oars. There are two main types: the lesser water boatman sieves organic matter from the water via hairs on its legs (it also uses its legs to rub together at mating time, rather like the grasshopper). The greater water boatman meanwhile is a predator, and can give we mere humans a painful bite.

RICH DIVERSITY OF LIFE: THE BADDIES

There are always a few unwelcome pond visitors as well, but fortunately they are not numerous. These are possibly the worst two:

LEECHES

These suck the bodily fluids out of their prey. To avoid getting leeches in your pond, check any plants or fish that you introduce – wherever they come from. Most species feed on water snails and fish.

MOSQUITOES

These prefer still waters to ponds with waterfalls and fountains, and will lay their eggs anywhere that is still, even in long-standing puddles and waterbutts. Fortunately the eggs and larvae are considered delicious by fish, so you will often find greater populations of mosquitoes where there is an absence of fish.

ABOVE **Leeches must be the most unpopular of all pond inhabitants**

Year-round maintenance

I t is one thing to create a wonderful pond or water feature but, unless you are prepared to tend it and maintain it, there is very little point. Add to this the welfare of the fish, plants and wildlife that rely on the pond being kept in good condition, and you can see that a programme of regular activity is essential. Indeed, a monthly schedule – or seasonal schedule at the very least – is ideal. This chapter will set you on the right course.

EARLY WINTER

PREVENTING ICE

Unless you live in a mild area, the water in your pond is likely to freeze over at some time during the winter, but there are precautions you can take to prevent this.

ABOVE Electric pond heaters – which keep areas of the pond surface from freezing – comprise a straight rod element and a float

Rubber balls: some gardeners like to float a rubber ball in the pond. The theory is that the movement of the ball in the water, combined with the fact·that the air within the ball is at a higher temperature than the water itself, prevents ice from forming within the vicinity. This is the cheapest method but, in reality, it very often fails to work at all, with the ball icing up and sticking fast. Also, it has to be said, a rubber ball on the surface of the water doesn't look particularly fetching.

Running water: keep a section of the pond free from ice by running a fountain or waterfall permanently. The theory is that the moving water does not become still enough for ice to form. Without doubt this is the most successful method for keeping patches of pond surface ice-free. However, it is less effective in really severe winter cold, and of course there is a cost in terms of the electricity bill and wear and tear on the pump.

Electric heaters: if you have a power supply laid on for a pump, installing an electric pool heater becomes an easy and reliable option. It will usually comprise a straight rod element fitted through a wooden or polystyrene float which keeps the heater at surface level. It is plugged in directly to the mains supply and left in position whenever hard frost is forecast. Very effective, and not particularly expensive. However, if your pool has already iced over, you could try the boiling pan remedy.

Boiling pan: place a saucepan full of boiling water on the ice to melt a hole. If the ice is more than ½in (1cm) thick, and the saucepan is of average weight and thickness, it can take five minutes or more to melt the hole, so it is a bit like watching paint dry. To provide the pond with enough 'holes' to prevent the build-up of noxious gases in the water, can take several hours of to-ing and fro-ing with boiling pans. And the whole process needs to take place again the following day!

Never, ever, use a hammer, boot, screwdriver, elbow, or crowbar to break the ice. Although effective, the shockwaves and reverberation could stun or even kill the animal and fish life in your pond.

CREATE A FISH SANCTUARY

If your pond is on the small side and has little greenery in winter, there may be nowhere for your fish to hide. This in itself will do them no harm, but it does mean that they have nowhere to dart if a heron or a cat appears. To create a sanctuary, you can cut some short lengths of black plastic pipe and gently drop them into the pool. They won't be obtrusive, but could make the difference between life and death for the fish.

OTHER WATER GARDEN JOBS FOR EARLY WINTER

- Plan new ponds or water features
- Remove blanketweed and any other forms of algae
- Choose a mild, still day to pot on any pondside container plants that have outgrown their current pot
- Clear the pond of any autumn leaves that have fallen from nearby trees or shrubs

ABOVE **If goldfish are taking food in early winter, give them a bit more — but do not oversupply it**

MID-WINTER

CHECK OVERWINTERING PLANTS

Tender pond plants such as water hyacinth (*Eichhornia*), that were lifted in autumn for storing indoors or under glass, should be inspected every two weeks or more during winter. The atmosphere and heat in which they are being kept will determine whether or not they need watering or misting – sometimes misting over the tops of the plants is all that they require. As winter progresses, they will need checking more often for signs of life, and may need to be moved to a lighter or warmer position.

FISH

Many pond-keepers stop feeding their fish completely in winter, while others believe that if the weather is mild and the fish are active, their reserves will be depleted if they don't eat.

If the fish are swimming close to the surface, offer them a sprinkling of food. If they take it, give them a little more; if they decline, then stop.

WHAT'S LOOKING GOOD NOW IN THE GARDEN?
Water garden & bog plants:
Umbrella plant (*Cyperus involucratus*)
Water hawthorn (*Aponogeton distachyos*)
Various grasses, rushes and sedges

Other garden flowers:
Anemone, Chionodoxa, Crocus, Cyclamen, Eranthis, Erythronium, Galanthus, Helleborus, Iris, Saxifraga, Scilla and 'Universal' winter pansies

OTHER WATER GARDEN JOBS FOR MID-WINTER
◆ All jobs as for early winter
◆ Weed the bog garden
◆ On mild days, plant new trees and shrubs along the water's edge, or in the bog garden
◆ Take care not to disturb hibernating wildlife

ABOVE **A mid-winter bloomer –** *Crocus vernus* '**Pickwick**'

LATE WINTER

EXCAVATION WORK

If you are thinking about making a new pond, or re-shaping or enlarging an existing one, this is a good time to do it. If the work is completed now, you will be able to start planting, and introducing fish in about six weeks, which will bring you nicely in to the early to mid-spring season.

The most important thing to bear in mind is the depth of your proposed pond. It must be at least 18in (45cm) deep, and preferably 2ft (60cm) or more, and digging to this depth can be quite difficult. However it will be worth it, for it will provide an extra volume of water for plants to root and thrive, and for fish to flourish.

For serious excavation work, either hire a small digger, or hold a pond-digging party for all your able-bodied friends!

WILDLIFE

At this time of year frogs are mating, and there will be an abundance of frog spawn and tadpoles as a result. It is important to ensure that any frogs – as well toads and newts – can escape from the pond when the time is right. If the sides of your pond are vertical, or the edges

ABOVE **Large clumps of frogspawn will appear now**

overhang the water, install a small ramp, so that they can escape. A small log, or plank, if discreetly positioned, is ideal.

OTHER WATER GARDEN JOBS FOR LATE WINTER

- ◆ Add oxygenators to your pond
- ◆ Lift and divide overgrown marginals
- ◆ Give waterlilies in under-water planters a feed by inserting tablets of fertilizer into the soil, next to the crown of the plant
- ◆ Top up water levels following the winter onslaught

ABOVE **Oxygenating plants can be added to ponds in winter**

WHAT'S LOOKING GOOD NOW IN THE GARDEN?

Water garden & bog plants:
Drumstick primula (*Primula denticulata*)
Water hawthorn (*Aponogeton distachyos*)

Other garden flowers:
Anemone, Chionodoxa, Crocus, Cyclamen, Eranthis, Erythronium, Fritillaria, Gentiana, Hyacinthus, Narcissus, Primula, Pulmonaria, Saxifraga, Scilla and *Tulipa*

EARLY SPRING

TAKE OUT THE DEBRIS

- Remove pond algae as and when you see it. It will flourish if left unchecked, and become entangled with more precious aquatic plants.
- Dead leaves should also be removed. Decaying vegetation will pollute the water and end up harming the fish. If a spring clean is necessary, a temporary home will need to be found for the fish.

FISH

Fish are cold-blooded, which means that they become more active as the temperature rises, and the fat reserves that sustained them during the winter will be exhausted now. With their resistance to infections at its lowest, fish need careful nurturing to restore their normal strength and energy and to improve their health generally in time for the breeding season. So, it's important to start feeding them, but don't use too much food or it will contaminate the water. Scatter a few pellets on the surface in the evening and add a few more if they take the first batch.

OTHER WATER GARDEN JOBS FOR EARLY SPRING

- Plant new plants in the bog garden
- Following the winter, it is a good idea to test the quality and pH of the water, and make any remedial treatments
- Feed containerized aquatic plants with appropriate pellets, and established bog

garden plants with general fertilizer, but do not allow any run-off to enter the pond
- Lift and divide overgrown marginals
- If you removed your submersible pump before the onset of winter (see mid-autumn, pages 85–87), now is the time to re-install it

ABOVE **Grape hyacinths (*Muscari armeniacum*)**

WHAT'S LOOKING GOOD NOW IN THE GARDEN?
Water garden & bog plants:
Arum italicum 'Marmoratum'
Arum lily (*Zantedeschia aethiopica*)
Bugle (*Ajuga reptans*)
Cotton grass (*Eriophorum angustifolium*)
Drumstick primula (*Primula denticulata*)
Water hawthorn (*Aponogeton distachyos*)

Other garden flowers:
Anemone, Bellis, Brunnera, Chionodoxa, Convallaria, Crocus, Cyclamen, Erysimum, Erythronium, Fritillaria, Gentiana, Hyacinthus, Iris, Leucojum, Muscari, Narcissus, Polygonatum, Primula, Scilla and *Tulipa*

ABOVE **If you empty your pond for a spring clean, fish will need a temporary home**

MID-SPRING

IN THE BOG GARDEN

Give the plants a little extra food now, but always use fertilizers with caution near a pond. When there is no wind, sprinkle a handful of fish, blood and bone powder around the base of the plants, rather than spraying liquid feed over them.

WHAT'S LOOKING GOOD NOW IN THE GARDEN?
Water garden & bog plants:
Arum italicum 'Marmoratum'
Arum lily (*Zantedeschia aethiopica*)
Astilbes
Bog bean (*Menyanthes trifoliata*)
Bugle (*Ajuga reptans*)
Candelabra primula (*Primula beesiana*)
Candelabra primula (*Primula japonica*)
Candelabra primula (*Primula pulverulenta*)
Cotton grass (*Eriophorum angustifolium*)
Drumstick primula (*Primula denticulata*)
Globe flower (*Trollius europaeus*)
Golden club (*Orontium aquaticum*)
Greater spearwort (*Ranunculus lingua* 'Grandiflorus')
Japanese water iris (*Iris laevigata*)
Marsh marigold (*Caltha palustris*)
Skunk cabbage (*Lysichiton americanus*)
Water avens (*Geum rivale*)
Water forget-me-not (*Myosotis scorpioides*)
Water violet (*Hottonia palustris*)
Yellow flag iris (*Iris pseudacorus*)

Other garden flowers:
Allium, Anemone, Aquilegia, Bellis, Convallaria, Cyclamen, Dicentra, Erysimum, Erythronium, Fritillaria, Gentiana, Hyacinthus, Leucojum, Muscari, Narcissus, Ornithogalum, Papaver, Polygonatum, Saxifraga, Trillium and *Tulipa*

ABOVE **Mid-spring, before growth begins apace, is the ideal time to divide, tidy up and re-pot waterlilies**

Stake any plants that are now putting on lush young growth at a fast rate. At this time of year it's best to use 'wrap-around' support, to avoid damaging the stems.

FISH

Watch your fish. At this time, as temperatures rise, fish begin to spawn. For several days the males will be seen pursuing and almost 'bullying' the females by chasing them into the denser patches of pondweed and it is there that the females will be stimulated to lay their tiny eggs.

OTHER WATER GARDEN JOBS FOR MID-SPRING

◆ Introduce new aquatic plants to your pond
◆ Divide overgrown waterlily clumps
◆ Watch for clusters of snails' eggs
◆ Rid your pond of algae and blanketweed – at this time it can be at its worst
◆ Check for signs of slugs on bog garden plants and marginals, and treat as appropriate

LATE SPRING

IN THE BOG GARDEN

◆ Now is a good time to tidy the bog garden and remove any dead or diseased foliage.

◆ Check to see if plants that flower in early or mid-spring are affected by mildew – just think of forget-me-nots. By cutting the affected parts hard back, you can encourage fresh new growth and perhaps a new crop of flowers later in the summer.

◆ Dead heading is also important. Apart from making the plant less ugly it removes any areas where mould can set in. Never forget that by its nature a bog garden is damp all of the time and botrytis, grey mould and similar diseases may be more troublesome here than elsewhere in the garden.

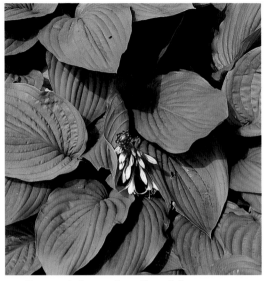

ABOVE **Hostas are looking good now. This is** *H. fortunaei aurea*

WHAT'S LOOKING GOOD NOW IN THE GARDEN?

Water garden & bog plants:
Arum italicum 'Marmoratum'
Arum lily (*Zantedeschia aethiopica*)
Bog arum (*Calla palustris*)
Bog bean (*Menyanthes trifoliata*)
Brass buttons (*Cotula coronopifolia*)
Bugle (*Ajuga reptans*)
Candelabra primula (*Primula beesiana*)
Candelabra primula (*Primula japonica*)
Candelabra primula (*Primula pulverulenta*)
Common water plantain (*Alisma plantago*)
Sweet flag (*Acorus calamus*)
Flowering rush (*Butomus umbellatus*)
Giant prickly rhubarb (*Gunnera manicata*)
Globe flower (*Trollius europaeus*)
Golden club (*Orontium aquaticum*)
Greater spearwort (*Ranunculus lingua* 'Grandiflorus')
Himalayan cowslip (*Primula florindae*)
Houttuynia cordata 'Chameleon'
Marsh marigold (*Caltha palustris*)

Musk flower (*Mimulus luteus*)
Ornamental rhubarb (*Rheum palmatum*)
Riverside windflower (*Anemone rivularis*)
Rodgersia podophylla
Skunk cabbage (*Lysichiton americanus*)
Water avens (*Geum rivale*)
Water forget-me-not (*Myosotis scorpioides*)
Water violet (*Hottonia palustris*)
Various *Astilbe, Hemerocallis, Hosta* and water irises

Other garden flowers:
Various bedding, including *Ageratum, Begonia, Pelargonium, Godetia, Impatiens, Mesembryanthemum, Nicotiana, Tagetes* and *Viola*.
Various herbaceous perennials and bulbs, including *Acanthus, Allium, Campanula, Delphinium, Dianthus, Erigeron, Geranium, Gladiolus, Lilium, Lupinus, Meconopsis, Papaver,* peonies, *Polygonatum, Phlox* and *Saxifraga*

◆ A well-made bog garden should be moist for most of the time, but in prolonged periods of hot, dry weather, the ground – and therefore the plants – can sometimes need extra help. In the evening, use a garden sprinkler to thoroughly wet the area. A permanently installed trickle irrigation system would be an even better idea, as you would simply have to turn on the tap for a period of time.

FISH

◆ If your pond fish have spawned, make sure that the fry have access to a shallow area, safe from the attentions of adult fish who will consider them as tasty morsels.
◆ If the water has reached 70°F (15°C), you could transfer some of your tropical fish from indoor aquaria to the pond for the duration of the summer.

OTHER WATER GARDEN JOBS FOR LATE SPRING

◆ All jobs as for mid-spring
◆ Check for signs of plant pests, such as aphids, and treat as appropriate
◆ Control the spread of duckweed, or your pond could be covered by the end of summer

EARLY SUMMER

EVAPORATION

After a few days of hot weather water gardeners everywhere are asking themselves if their ponds have sprung a leak. In most cases, they won't have but it's surprising how much water can be lost through evaporation on a really hot day. This is particularly important with small water features such as water barrels or wall-mounted fountains. Not only does the pond look less attractive, but life begins to be pretty uncomfortable for the amphibia in it, too. It is, therefore, important to keep the water level topped up regularly. A fine-spray attachment on the end of a hose is ideal, otherwise the pool will be churned up and

plants disturbed. If you have an open-ended hose, allow the water to trickle into the pond.

First, however, check that your local water company regulations allow you to use a hose in this way. Although hand-held hoses are generally still acceptable, increasingly there is a requirement to have a water meter installed if you want to leave a hose unattended for any length of time.

FISH

In really hot weather, the water becomes comparatively warm and the fish can become lethargic. Feeding should be reduced slightly during the warmest periods.

OTHER WATER GARDEN JOBS FOR EARLY SUMMER

◆ All jobs as for late spring
◆ Check whether any overgrown clumps of oxygenators and other fast-growing aquatics need to be thinned
◆ Weed the bog garden, and apply copious amounts of water during dry spells
◆ Check and prune waterlilies

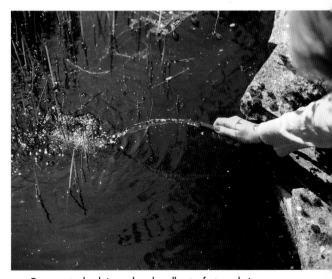

ABOVE **Top up water levels in ponds and small water features during hot weather**

WHAT'S LOOKING GOOD NOW IN THE GARDEN?

Water garden & bog plants:
Arrow arum (*Peltandra undulata*)
Arrowhead (*Sagittaria sagittifolia*)
Arum lily (*Zantedeschia aethiopica*)
Bog arum (*Calla palustris*)
Bog bean (*Menyanthes trifoliata*)
Branched bur-reed (*Sparganium erectum*)
Brass buttons (*Cotula coronopifolia*)
Candelabra primula (*Primula beesiana*)
Common water plantain (*Alisma plantago*)
Chinese loosestrife (*Lysimachia clethroides*)
Flowering rush (*Butomus umbellatus*)
Giant prickly rhubarb (*Gunnera manicata*)
Globe flower (*Trollius europaeus*)
Goat's beard (*Aruncus dioicus*)
Golden club (*Orontium aquaticum*)
Greater spearwort (*Ranunculus lingua* 'Grandiflorus')
Himalayan cowslip (*Primula florindae*)
Houttuynia cordata 'Chameleon'
Lady's mantle (*Alchemilla mollis*)
Marsh marigold (*Caltha palustris*)
Musk flower (*Mimulus luteus*)
Ornamental rhubarb (*Rheum palmatum*)
Pickerel weed (*Pontederia cordata*)

Primula vialli
Purple monkey flower (*Mimulus lewisii*)
Ragged robin (*Lychnis flos-cuculi*)
Riverside windflower (*Anemone rivularis*)
Rodgersia aesculifolia
Skunk cabbage (*Lysichiton americanus*)
Sweet flag (*Acorus calamus*)
Water avens (*Geum rivale*)
Water forget-me-not (*Myosotis scorpioides*)
Water hawthorn (*Aponogeton distachyos*)
Water soldiers (*Stratiotes aloides*)
Water violet (*Hottonia palustris*)
Yellow pond lily (*Nuphar lutea*)
Various *Astilbe, Hemerocallis, Hosta*, water irises and *Nymphaea* (waterlily)

Other garden flowers:
Bedding as for late spring, with the addition of *Antirrhinum*, begonias, dahlias, *Lobelia, Petunia, Salvia* and stocks.
Herbaceous and bulbs as for late spring, with the addition of *Achillea, Kniphofia, Oenothera, Spiraea, Tropaeoloum* and *Verbascum*

MID-SUMMER

WISH YOU WERE HERE...

For most people high summer is the time for the annual holiday. Life in the pond won't actually come to a grinding halt if you're not there to tend to its every need for a couple of weeks, but there are a few things you could do to maintain optimum performance of water, plants and fish.

Ask a neighbour to switch on any aeration device (i.e. a fountain or a waterfall/cascade) for a short while during the period that you're away. This will help to oxygenate the water.

ABOVE **Feeding blocks can be used to provide your fish with nourishment while you are away**

WHAT'S LOOKING GOOD NOW IN THE GARDEN?

Water garden & bog plants:
Arrowhead (*Sagittaria sagittifolia*)
Arum lily (*Zantedeschia aethiopica*)
Bog pimpernel (*Anagallis tenella*)
Branched bur-reed (*Sparganium erectum*)
Brass buttons (*Cotula coronopifolia*)
Chinese loosestrife (*Lysimachia clethroides*)
Common water plantain (*Alisma plantago*)
Filipendula camtschatica
Frogbit (*Hydrocharis morsus-ranae*)
Giant prickly rhubarb (*Gunnera manicata*)
Goat's beard (*Aruncus dioicus*)
Golden club (*Orontium aquaticum*)
Greater spearwort (*Ranunculus lingua* 'Grandiflorus')
Houttuynia cordata 'Chameleon'
Lady's mantle (*Alchemilla mollis*)
Mare's tail (*Hippuris vulgaris*)
Marsh gentian (*Gentiana pneumonanthe*)
Marsh St John's wort (*Hypericum elodioides*)
Musk flower (*Mimulus luteus*)
Pickerel weed (*Pontaderia cordata*)
Purple monkey flower (*Mimulus lewisii*)
Ragged robin (*Lychnis flos-cuculi*)
Reed mace (*Typha latifolia*)
Rodgersia aesculifolia
Sweet flag (*Acorus calamus*)
Sweet galingale (*Cyperus longus*)
Water forget-me-not (*Myosotis scorpioides*)
Water fringe (*Nymphoides peltatum*)
Water hawthorn (*Aponogeton distachyos*)
Water hyacinth (*Eichhornia crassipes*)
Water mint (*Mentha aquatica*)
Water soldiers (*Stratiotes aloides*)
Water violet (*Hottonia palustris*)
Willow grass (*Persicaria amphibia*)
Yellow pond lily (*Nuphar lutea*)
Various *Astilbe, Hemerocallis, Hosta,* water irises and *Nymphaea* (waterlily)

ABOVE **The variegated reed mace (*Typha latifolia* 'Variegata')**

Other garden flowers:
Various bedding including *Ageratum, Alyssum, Antirrhinum, Begonia, Godetia, Impatiens, Lathyrus, Lobelia, Mesembryanthemum, Petunia, Salvia* and stocks.
Various herbaceous and bulbs including *Acanthus, Allium, Dahlia, Dianthus, Echinacea, Echinops, Erigeron, Gazania, Geum, Geranium, Gladiolus, Helenium, Helianthus, Helichrysum, Kniphofia, Lavatera, Liatris, Lilium, Oenothera, Papaver, Penstemon, Rudbeckia, Tigridia, Verbena* and *Verbascum*

ABOVE **Remove dead or damaged waterlily leaves before they rot**

However, if you don't have a powered aeration device, you could ask your neighbour to empty a bucket of clean water, or run a hosepipe into the pond on thundery days, and this will do some good.

Make sure any water plant seedlings and young plants you're in the course of propagating are covered with enough water in their trays, to stop them from dehydrating, and keep them out of the sun to reduce evaporation.

FISH

As long as there are plenty of water plants of all kinds in your pond, fish can generally manage for a couple of weeks without supplementary feeding. Block feeders are available for fish in ponds that have few plants. These blocks mainly comprise calcium impregnated with specially formulated fish food pellets.

Fish need oxygen, and the amount of oxygen in pond water decreases when the temperature rises. When the water temperature rises to 80°F (25°C) or higher, fish are likely to gulp air at the water's surface, or leave a bubbly froth in their wake. A fountain or waterfall will help to oxygenate the water, or simply run water from a hosepipe, agitating it around for a few minutes.

OTHER WATER GARDEN JOBS FOR MID-SUMMER

◆ All jobs as for early summer
◆ Remove the faded flowers from early summer-flowering bog garden plants (such as hemerocallis)
◆ Pond levels may still need topping up in warm weather
◆ Continue to remove blanketweed and other forms of algae

LATE SUMMER

TIDY, TIDY, TIDY...

After the warm summer months when the pond has sustained itself without too much human assistance, there is now a steady increase in the number of jobs needing to be done.

Plants are starting to die down and the rate of decline is faster than the rate of growth, so late summer is the time to start a weekly routine of pulling out dead leaves and stems from your pond, before they sink to the bottom. If you do not remove them, they will give off harmful gases but, if kept to just small quantities, the gases can escape from the pond and do little harm. Large quantities however can pollute the water, and during winter the pond may freeze over, so that the potentially toxic gases would build up under the ice, and the fish suffer.

YOUR WEEKLY TIDYING REGIME SHOULD BE AS FOLLOWS:

◆ Cut and clear away any collapsing stems and leaves before they enter the water.
◆ Trim back fading marginal plants by two-thirds (but don't cut them too low in case their hollow stems become totally submerged and rot).
◆ Leave one or two areas as cover for the various water animals that like to spend their winter in hiding near the banks.
◆ The older leaves of waterlilies will be looking increasingly ragged now. Either pull these away, or cut them with a sharp knife.

WHAT'S LOOKING GOOD NOW IN THE GARDEN?

Water garden & bog plants:
Arrowhead (*Sagittaria sagittifolia*)
Arum italicum 'Marmoratum'
Arum lily (*Zantedeschia aethiopica*)
Branched bur-reed (*Sparganium erectum*)
Brass buttons (*Cotula coronopifolia*)
Cardinal flower (*Lobelia cardinalis*)
Chinese loosestrife (*Lysimachia clethroides*)
Common water plantain (*Alisma plantago*)
Flowering rush (*Butomus umbellatus*)
Frogbit (*Hydrocharis morsus-ranae*)
Golden rays (*Ligularia dentata*)
Greater spearwort (*Ranunculus lingua* 'Grandiflorus')
Hemp agrimony (*Eupatorium cannabinum*)
Houttuynia cordata 'Chameleon'
Kirengeshoma palmata
Lady's mantle (*Alchemilla mollis*)
Lavender musk (*Mimulus ringens*)
Mare's tail (*Hippuris vulgaris*)
Marsh gentian (*Gentiana pneumonanthe*)
Marsh St John's wort (*Hypericum elodioides*)
Meadowsweet (*Filipendula ulmaria*)

Pickerel weed (*Pontaderia cordata*)
Purple monkey flower (*Mimulus lewisii*)
Reed mace (*Typha latifolia*)
Sweet flag (*Acorus calamus*)
Water hawthorn (*Aponogeton distachyos*)
Water hyacinth (*Eichhornia crassipes*)
Water mint (*Mentha aquatica*)
Water fringe (*Nymphoides peltatum*)
Water soldiers (*Stratiotes aloides*)
Willow grass (*Persicaria amphibia*)
Yellow pond lily (*Nuphar lutea*)

Other garden flowers:
Achillea, Aconitum, Agapanthus, Anemone x hybrida, Arctotis, Aster (Michaelmas daisy), autumn gentian, *Canna, Chrysanthemum, Colchicum, Crinum, Cyclamen, Dahlia, Echinops, Erigeron, Felicia, Gazania, Gladiolus, Geranium, Helianthus, Impatiens, Ipomoea, Kniphofia, Lavatera, Liatris, Mesembry-anthemum, Monarda, Nicotiana, Penstemon, Phlox, Physostegia, Rudbeckia, Schizostylus, Sedum, Solidago* and *Verbena*

If the ragged leaves are just out of normal reach, attach a razor blade to a cane. It will make a fine cutting tool.

◆ Keep an eye out for the two main waterlily pests: aphids and lily beetle. The aphids (also known as blackfly or greenfly) are instantly recognizable. The lily beetles are brown and small (as beetles go). You will see the damage created by the beetles: they nibble at the leaves causing holes in the middle and on the edges. Fire a jet of water at the leaves to knock the pests in to the water, and remove the worst-affected leaves.

ABOVE **Dead head all perennial and bog garden plants – here faded hemerocallis blooms are being removed**

ABOVE **Running a waterfall will help oxygenate water for fish**

FROGS

Decaying organic matter in the pond can pollute the water very quickly and frogs seem to be very reactive to the problem at this time of year. These amphibians are already suffering from widespread habitat loss and a serious bacterial ailment that has killed off huge populations in recent years ('red leg' – so named because there is a pronounced reddening of the legs). The bacterium thrives in water that is low in oxygen, so remove dying plant matter from the pond immediately.

OTHER WATER GARDEN JOBS FOR LATE SUMMER

- Divide overgrown marginal plants before the soil and water are too cold for replanting
- Detach young portions of tender aquatic plants (such as the water hyacinth, *Eichhornia*) for overwintering safely indoors
- Tropical or tender fish that have been enjoying the summer outdoors should be returned to their winter quarters indoors, particularly if the water temperature falls below 60°F (15°C)

EARLY AUTUMN

THE GREAT DIVIDE

Perennial plants in the bog garden can be lifted and divided both in spring and autumn, and now is as good a time to tackle all but the most tender perennials, which are better left until the spring.

Water and waterside plants tend to be more vigorous than their drier garden counterparts which means that you need to divide them rather

WHAT'S LOOKING GOOD NOW IN THE GARDEN?
Water garden & bog plants:
Arum italicum 'Marmoratum'
Bladderwort (*Utricularia vulgaris*)
Bugbane (*Cimicifuga simplex*)
Brass buttons (*Cotula coronopifolia*)
Cardinal flower (*Lobelia cardinalis*)
Greater spearwort (*Ranunculus lingua* 'Grandiflorus')
Marsh St John's wort (*Hypericum elodioides*)
Pickerel weed (*Pontaderia cordata*)
Purple monkey flower (*Mimulus lewisii*)
Reed mace (*Typha latifolia*)
Umbrella plant (*Cyperus involucratus*)
Water fringe (*Nymphoides peltatum*)
Water hawthorn (*Aponogeton distachyos*)
Water hyacinth (*Eichhornia crassipes*)
Willow grass (*Persicaria amphibia*)

Other garden flowers:
Aconitum, Anemone, Aster, Ceratostigma, Chrysanthemum, Colchicum, Cortaderia, Crocus, Cyclamen, Gaillardia, Galanthus, Gentiana, Geum, Helianthus, Kniphofia, Liriope, Nerine, Penstemon, Rudbeckia, Sedum, Solidago, Sternbergia, Stokesia and *Verbena*

more frequently – pull apart large clumps and discard the tough older centres, replanting only the more vigorous, outer sections.

Don't be tempted to lift waterlilies and other fully aquatic species now – they should be left until spring.

MARGINAL CUT-BACKS

Many clumps of marginal species will have spent the summer trying to march their way across the pond and reclaim the open water. They must now be cut back.

Whereas perennial plants in dry soil should be cut back to just above ground level, it's best to leave marginal species with rather longer stumps, especially if they are a trifle tender and have hollow stems; otherwise the accumulation of water within the stem bases – which will freeze during winter – can cause damage and allow rot to penetrate the crown.

FISH

It is now that fish need to build up their food reserves. Being cold-blooded, they will be fairly inactive during the depths of winter, and their survival will depend on what they have eaten during summer and autumn.

Continue to feed them regularly, but it is even more important from now on that you make sure they eat all that is given to them. Excess food will drop to the bottom and rot, so scatter a few flakes or pellets and supply more only if the first are completely devoured.

OTHER WATER GARDEN JOBS FOR EARLY AUTUMN

◆ Continue to remove blanketweed and other forms of algae
◆ As daylight lengths shorten, thin floating plants (such as duckweed and *Azolla*) to allow as much sunlight on to the pond as possible
◆ Scoop out from the pond any fallen leaves or rotting plant material

ABOVE **Water lettuce (*Pistia stratiotes*) needs to be overwintered in a frost-free environment**

◆ Detach young portions of tender aquatic plants (such as *Eichhornia* and *Pistia*, the water lettuce) for overwintering safely indoors
◆ It is your last chance to return to their winter quarters indoors any tropical or tender fish that have been outside during the summer, particularly if the water temperature falls below 60°F (15°C)

MID-AUTUMN

PUMP CARE

Most owners of ponds with moving water have submersible pumps, and there is a school of thought which proclaims that these should not only be left in the water all year round, but that they should also be working, pumping round the water 24 hours a day, 365 days a year.

During really cold weather the water movement, or 'agitation', that these pumps provide ensures that the pool has at least a small area free from ice.

If you prefer to remove the pump and store it over winter, then now is the time to disconnect it. Clean it out as best you can, as well as the associated pipework. Surface pumps, in any case, will need to be so treated at this time.

LEAF COLLECTION

Continue to remove leaves from the pond or water feature. As autumn progresses, the greater the likelihood that ignored leaves will sink to the bottom of the pond, so be prepared to delve into the depths with your net or, even better, your hand. Try not to disturb the mud too much, as many creatures will be hibernating in it.

SPRING BULBS

Small bulbs look extremely attractive when planted close to water, and this is the latest time to plant them if you want flowers next spring. Smaller narcissi, crocuses, snowdrops, muscari and scillas are particularly effective – avoid the

ABOVE **Mid-autumn is the right time to disconnect and clean submersible pumps**

ABOVE **Small bulbs look good when planted near to water – plant them during autumn**

WHAT'S LOOKING GOOD NOW IN THE GARDEN?
Water garden & bog plants:
Purple monkey flower (*Mimulus lewisii*)
Royal fern (*Osmunda regalis*)
Umbrella plant (*Cyperus involucratus*)
Water hawthorn (*Aponogeton distachyos*)
Willow grass (*Persicaria amphibia*)
Various grasses, rushes and sedges

Other garden flowers:
Aconitum, Anemone, Aster, Ceratostigma, Chrysanthemum, Colchicum, Cortaderia, Crocus, Cyclamen, Galanthus, Gentiana, Helenium, Rudbeckia, Schizostylis, Sedum and *Sternbergia*

larger varieties of bulbs (daffodils, tulips and hyacinths particularly) as they look inappropriate in this situation.

If your pool is formal, then the bulbs are best planted in containers (but do ensure that the new pots you're using are guaranteed to be frost-proof). If your pond is informal, then the bulbs are best planted into nearby beds – although not directly into a bog garden, where they are likely to rot.

CONTAINER PLANTS

Growing perennial plants, as well as trees and shrubs, in containers close to more formal pools makes a great deal of sense – you can't, after all, plant into paving stones! If the weather is still fairly mild, as it often is at this time of year, there is no harm in repotting some of the bigger specimens into slightly larger containers now.

OTHER WATER GARDEN JOBS FOR MID-AUTUMN

◆ Continue to remove blanketweed and other forms of algae

ABOVE **Use old leaves of *Gunnera* to cover the crowns over winter**

- Continue to thin floating plants to allow as much sunlight on to the pond as possible
- Last chance to cover and protect any tender marginal or bog garden plants before the worst of the weather sets in
- Take hardwood cuttings of any pondside trees and shrubs

LATE AUTUMN

PREPARE FOR THE FUTURE

This is a good time to start a new pond (or extend existing ones), free from the urgency of spring, the heat and dryness of summer and the cold and inhospitable ground conditions of winter. The weather now is usually warm enough to make the work pleasant, while the risk of prolonged frost is still slight.

If you are contemplating a new pond, before any practical work is carried out you must decide on its location. Remember the golden rules for pond positioning:

- Do place ponds in full sun
- Do place ponds on level sites
- Do not place ponds under trees
- Do not place ponds at the foot of slopes

FISH

Around now the water in the pond will reach 40°F (5°C), the critical point below which all feeding of fish should stop.

OTHER WATER GARDEN JOBS FOR LATE AUTUMN

- All jobs as for mid-autumn
- Check your liner (or concrete) above the waterline for cracks and leaks
- Check for slippery paths and paving stones around the edge of the pond – these can be lethal
- Prevent ice forming (see early winter, on page 72)
- Reflect on the year gone by and what might have gone wrong

ABOVE **The umbrella plant (*Cyperus involucratus*)**

WHAT'S LOOKING GOOD NOW IN THE GARDEN?

Water garden & bog plants:
Royal fern (*Osmunda regalis*)
Umbrella plant (*Cyperus involucratus*)
Water hawthorn (*Aponogeton distachyos*)
Various grasses, rushes and sedges

Other garden flowers:
Autumn crocus, Cyclamen, Galanthus, Helleborus, Iris unguicularis, Schizostylis and *Sternbergia*

LEFT A water garden, even a fairly
intricate one with running water,
cascades and built-in shelves, is
bland without the plants

TYPICAL PLANT
HARDINESS ZONES FOR
WESTERN EUROPE

New forms of temperate, moisture-loving and aquatic green plants are being developed all the time, mainly for flower colour, flower longevity and pest and disease resistance. But often it is hardiness, and other weather tolerances, that is bred into them. So it is useful to know, when buying your plants, which climate suits them best – the parts of the world in which they originated usually dictate this – but it

is not exclusively the case. If you live in Europe or the US, the maps on these pages will give you an indication of the plant hardiness zones for where you live. As you will see from the Directory section that follows, aquatic and moisture-loving plants are quite adaptable, so wherever you live you should be able to find a selection of good plants that suit you, your pond's and your garden's requirements.

TYPICAL PLANT HARDINESS ZONES FOR NORTH AMERICA

Keys to colours (both maps)

- Zone 1: below −50°F (−46°C)
- Zone 2: −50 to −40°F (−46 to −40°C)
- Zone 3: −40 to −30°F (−40 to −34.5°C)
- Zone 4: −30 to −20°F (−34 to −29°C)
- Zone 5: −20 to −10°F (−29 to −23°C)
- Zone 6: −10 to 0°F (−23 to −18°C)
- Zone 7: 0 to 10°F (−18 to −12°C)
- Zone 8: 10 to 20°F (−12 to −7°C)
- Zone 9: 20 to 30°F (−7 to −1°C)
- Zone 10: 30 to 40°F (−1 to 4°C)
- Zone 11: above 40°F (above 4°C)

HOW TO USE THESE MAPS

Each entry in the plant directory lists the relevant zones where it should be possible to grow the plant successfully, based on these heat-zone maps. Find your location on the map, and you can then identify the zone that your area belongs to. Do not forget to take into account that cities are warmer than rural locations.

CHAPTER 9

A–Z plant directory

This plant directory does not claim to be an exhaustive list but it does contain a selection of some of the best plants for furnishing your water garden. The plants are listed alphabetically within the section that relates to their type (floating water plants, flowering water plants, marginal and bog garden plants).

FLOATING WATER PLANTS

Floating water plants are those that are not anchored by roots, although some do produce a few straggly roots that simply dangle in the water. These plants tend to die down during late autumn, surviving the winter as dormant 'buds', resting in the mud at the bottom of the pond. In spring, when the weather warms, they burst into life again.

FLOWERING WATER PLANTS

Aquatic plants come into a number of different categories, such as oxygenating and floating types, for instance. The flowering water plant is another category, and is somewhat larger than these two. These are plants that grow within the pond, anchored in the mud, or in planting containers, but which have leaves and flowers sitting on top of the water or rising above it.

Waterlilies are the classic flowering water plant but, like other plants in their group, varieties must be chosen very carefully, according to the vigour of their surface spread and the depth of water to which they are most suited.

MARGINAL PLANTS

My definition of a marginal plant may fly in the face of botanical purists, but at least it is unequivocal as far as the average (and beginner) gardener is concerned: a 'marginal', to my mind, is any plant that grows at the very edge of the water, regardless of the moisture content of the soil in which it's growing. This means that the marginals discussed in this directory will require a wide range of habitats, spanning all soil conditions, from permanently under water to semi-dry. If we are not careful, however, marginal plants will graduate, almost imperceptibly, into bog garden plants.

BOG PLANTS

The bog garden, although not a water garden in the purest form, does have a place in this book: at one end of the bog plant list are those species that like to be almost in the water, and are therefore just slightly removed from the marginals; at the other end there are those plants that require merely a consistently moist soil.

As sweeping generalizations go, bog garden plants tend to dislike dry, clay soil which resembles concrete in hot summers, and tend not to perform well if they are in a position exposed to high winds and the full strength of the sun all day long. Other than that, they enjoy a wide and varied selection of growing conditions.

THE NAMING OF PLANTS

Plants may be known by their common names but they are classified by their Latin (or botanical) names. Each plant is classified by at least two words.

The genus, or first name, refers to a group of plants with similar botanical features. For example: *hemerocallis*, which is the Latin name for the day lily. The species, or second name, is a descriptive name for the plant, so *Hemerocallis multiflora* describes a very floriferous day lily.

Sometimes you will see a cross between the names. This refers to an interspecific hybrid which is the result of crossing two related species within the same genus. For example: *Astilbe* x *arendsii*, which is a cross between two different astilbes and has larger plumes.

A cultivar is produced by plant breeding and may result, for example, in different coloured or larger flowers, disease resistance or variegated foliage. This is written after the species and is not in Latin. For example: *Rheum palmatum* 'Atrosanguineum', which has deep red leaves. When the cultivar is particularly distinct and further removed from the original species, it is used straight after the genus. For example: *Nymphaea* 'Paul Hariot'.

A slight variation in the species which occurs naturally is termed a variety. For example: *Nuphar japonica* var. *variegata*, which has variegated leaves instead of the usual green.

FLOATING WATER PLANTS

COMMON DUCKWEED (*LEMNA MINOR*)

Type Very hardy, one-species plant, tolerating temperatures as low as −4°F (−20°C). Duckweed survives in winter as dormant buds on the bottom of the pond.

Origin The Atlantic side of North America.

USDA zone Z4

Description The form that is generally found in garden ponds is *Lemna minor* and, if you introduce it to your pond – either accidentally or on purpose – the pond will soon be covered with a pale lime-green 'carpet'.

Flowers These appear in summer, and are tiny, grey-white and wholly insignificant.

Leaves Minute, almost translucent, deciduous fronds in various shapes, but mostly oval. Thousands of them abut each other to form a dense carpet over the surface of the water. Each individual frond usually produces a single, dangling root.

Cultivation One doesn't really 'cultivate' duckweed – it just happens! Planting comprises simply dropping several leaves with roots into the pond, generally in spring. It grows best in still, or nearly still water, and in either full sun or light shade. Duckweed is left to its own devices. All you need to do is use a net to thin it out occasionally to prevent it from covering and choking the whole pond.

Propagation Again, one doesn't really 'propagate' duckweed. Just redistribute some of the fronds to a different pond.

Height None – to speak of.

Spread A couple of individual fronds can increase and cover up to 9sq ft (1m²) in a year, but thereafter rapid covering of ponds can take place. Further spread should be controlled.

Recommended pond size Small – up to about 18sq ft (2m²).

Recommended water depth 6in (15cm).

Alternative plants Perhaps the best form to choose is the ivy-leaved duckweed (*Lemna trisulca*), which is less invasive than the common kind. It produces a mass of star-shaped leaves.

These leaves frequently float just beneath the surface. *Lemna gibba*, often referred to as the 'thick' or 'gibbous' duckweed, has rounded, swollen leaves and is particularly invasive. *Lemna polyrhiza* (also known as *Spirodela polyrhiza*, and commonly referred to as 'great' duckweed) has larger, rounder leaves than the normal kinds, and each has a small 'tuft' of roots attached. It is very invasive.

Tip Most gardening experts are asked how to get rid of duckweed, rather than how to grow it. Be warned: if you don't want it, it is important to check carefully each new water plant for the presence of duckweed before it is introduced to the pond.

FAIRY MOSS (*AZOLLA FILICULOIDES*)

Type Barely hardy, tolerating temperatures down to 23°F (−5°C) only.
Origin The warmer parts of North America.
USDA zone Z7
Description While this is no moss, neither is it a flowering plant. Actually, it is a charming tiny fern that congregates into dense masses. Although it is a native of more temperate climes, it survives quite harsh winters successfully. The simple, short and slender roots absorb nourishment from the pond water. Keeping multiplication under control in a small pond is not a problem but, as plants can eventually cover the whole surface, you should not

ABOVE **Duckweed – one doesn't really plant it, it just happens**

introduce this into large inaccessible ponds. It will rapidly get out of hand and become a nuisance.

Flowers None.

Leaves Pale blue-green lacy deciduous fronds, only ½in (1cm) across, turning a rich reddish-purple during autumn.

Cultivation In spring drop a few fronds directly onto the water. Best position is in full sun to light shade. This plant is unreliable in moving water such as caused by a fountain or waterfall. Net out unwanted plants during the growing season. Plants survive winter as submerged dormant buds, but as frost injury is possible some plantlets should be overwintered under glass in a jar of water and soil and kept frost-free.

Propagation Simply remove a few fronds and introduce them to a new pond during mid-spring.

Height Up to 1in (2.5cm).

Spread Prolific: a single piece can completely cover a small pond within a season.

Recommended pond size Small to medium – about 27sq ft (3m²) so that it can be controlled with the use of nets.

Alternative plants The normal species only is available, and it may sometimes be found under the name *Azolla caroliniana*.

Tip Azolla makes a useful addition to tropical aquaria but will need to be controlled regularly.

FROGBIT (*HYDROCHARIS MORSUS-RANAE*)

Type Tolerates temperatures as low as –4°F (–20°C); survives the winter as dormant buds.

Origin Northern Europe.

USDA zone Z4

Description The flowers of this plant look as if they are trilliums – woodland-dwelling plants with only three petals. However, frogbit is a rather beautiful floating aquatic plant. In its native countries it can, if not kept in check, quickly overcrowd and block up small pools, lakes and rivers.

Flowers From mid- to late summer, rising above the surface of the water, white three-petalled flowers appear, each with a yellow centre.

ABOVE **Azolla fills the available area, then pushes up into ridges to form an impenetrable mat**

95

Leaves Small, deciduous, rounded or kidney-shaped leaves of green-bronze leaves, both floating and raised above the water surface.

Cultivation 'Planting' consists of simply dropping young plants in the water; this should be done in spring. The best light conditions for frogbit are full sun to very light shade. Thin out established plants several times a year with a net to limit the spread. Water snails have a liking for the leaves, but this is the only problem you are likely to encounter.

Propagation Carefully remove young plantlets that form on runners (which are rather like strawberries, but on a much smaller scale). This is something that can be done at any time during the growing season.

Height Up to 2in (5cm).

Spread One plant will cover about 9sq ft (1m²) after a year.

Recommended pond size Small – to about 27sq ft (3m²).

Alternative plants Normally only this species is available.

Tip Frogbit is always best grown in a still pond, with water that is neutral to alkaline.

WATER HYACINTH (*EICHHORNIA CRASSIPES*)

Type Evergreen or semi-evergreen perennial. A tender plant which will tolerate temperatures only down to 59°F (15°C).

Origin Tropical South America.

USDA zone Z10

Description This robust free-floating plant is a prolific grower in hot climates. It flowers during late summer – the more flowers the hotter the summer. Although recommended for the garden pond in summer, it is a plant well suited to indoor water displays and large aquaria. It is so invasive in its natural, tropical habitat, that in some parts there are movement orders against it; in the US, federal law forbids shipping it between certain states.

Flowers Bluish-violet blooms, not unlike small hyacinths, rise above the water surface from mid-summer to early autumn.

Leaves Round, dark and shiny, almost succulent, with strong swollen stems honeycombed inside for buoyancy.

Cultivation Plant water hyacinths in early summer, by placing them into the pond. They perform best in full sun; the more sunlight that

ABOVE The water hyacinth (*Eichhornia crassipes*) is a worthy pond plant – but it is tender

beats down upon them, the better they like it. Invasiveness only becomes a problem if the plants are growing in very small ponds. Individual plants can be removed by hand if necessary.

Propagation Water hyacinths may be propagated by separating the clumps in spring, or in the autumn as they are removed to their winter quarters.

Height Up to 12in (30cm).

Spread Up to 9sq ft (1m²) per year.

Minimum pond size Tiny: even a water barrel or indoor aquarium could sustain a plant or two, but be prepared to thin them out regularly.

Alternative name It is sometimes sold as *Pontaderia crassipes*.

Tip Plants are most unlikely to survive a cold winter outdoors, so remove them from the pond during mid-autumn. Divide them, and store them in wet mud or moist pots in a greenhouse or cold frame until the spring. They can be re-sited in the pond from mid-spring onwards, but it is worth hardening them off gradually; the plant tissue will have become tender, and could be damaged if there is a severe late frost.

WATER SOLDIERS (*STRATIOTES ALOIDES*)

Type Semi-evergreen perennial. Fully hardy – to 5°F (–15°C).

Origin Europe

USDA zone Z5

Description This intriguing plant is often described as resembling a floating pineapple top. It is free-floating and held partly below and partly above the water. Curiously, plants sink and multiply after flowering, and rise again some weeks later, when surplus offsets can be thinned with a net. *Stratiotes* is a good choice for wildlife ponds. Prefers alkaline or limestone waters (which is why it does not always transfer from one pond to another successfully).

Flowers Early to late summer. Separate male and female forms, small, creamy white and papery, tucked in the leaf axils. The male

ABOVE **Water soldiers (*Stratiotes aloides*)**

flowers are produced in clusters in a pinkish spathe.

Leaves Dark olive green, narrow and stiff-toothed, arranged in neat rosettes.

Cultivation Water soldiers perform best in full sun. They usually overwinter at the bottom of the pond. *Stratiotes* can be prolific, but because the individual plants are so large, they can be removed by hand if necessary.

Propagation New plants form as small water buds on spreading stems: they may be propagated by separating the clumps in spring and summer.

Height Up to 19in (48cm).

Spread 3sq ft (0.4m²) per year.

Recommended pond size Small: up to about 18sq ft (2m²).

Preferred water depth 15–36in (38–90cm).

Alternative name Water aloe.

WATER VIOLET (*HOTTONIA PALUSTRIS*)

Type Herbaceous perennial. Very hardy, tolerating temperatures down to −4°F (−20°C).
Origin Britain, Northern Europe and Northern Asia.
USDA zone Z6

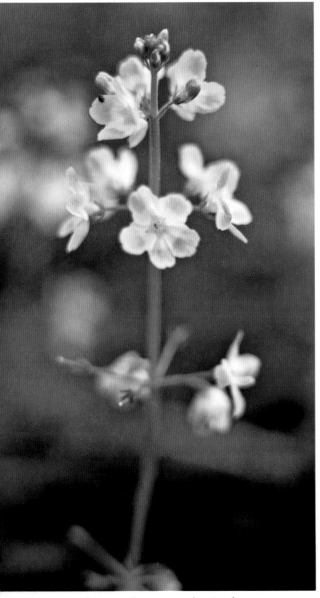

ABOVE **The water violet (*Hottonia palustris*) prefers to grow in still waters**

Description If you want to grow a floating water plant with attractive flowers held well above the surface of the water, and which doubles as an oxygenator, then you can hardly do better than to choose the water violet. This beautiful plant is not a violet at all, but a member of the primula family – and a fairly rare member at that. The flowers, when combined with leaves that protrude out of the water, give this plant the appearance of a marginal.

Flowers Spikes of white or pale lilac flowers 9in (23cm) high, in early to mid-summer.

Leaves The mid-green feathery leaves which float just below the surface of the water are efficient oxygenators, whilst other less divided leaves are also under the water, but do not oxygenate.

Cultivation These plants grow best in full sun or medium shade. Individual plants are dropped into the water in spring. In shallow water they will root in the mud at the bottom, but in deeper water will rest just below the surface – at least for the early part of the summer – before throwing up the flower spikes. Thin out excessive growth during the summer. In autumn plants die down and pass the winter as dormant buds, known as turions.

Propagation In summer. Divide larger plants, or root stem cuttings in wet mud. Gather any submerged seeds in autumn and grow them on in trays of mud.

Height Up to 15in (38cm).

Spread Will cover up to 3sq ft (1m²) per year.

Minimum water depth 6–18in (15–45cm).

Recommended pond size Small: up to about 18sq ft (2m²).

Alternative plants *Hottonia inflata* – referred to as the featherfoil – is similar, but is smaller, with white flowers. However, it is a rare plant and it is difficult to find a supplier.

Tip The water violet prefers still, rather than moving water, so it is best to avoid growing this plant in ponds that are fed by cascades or which contain fountains.

FLOWERING WATER PLANTS

BRANCHED BUR-REED (*SPARGANIUM ERECTUM*)

Type Very hardy, tolerating temperatures as low as −4°F (−20°C).

Origin Evidence exists that this plant is native to Europe from the Arctic Circle downwards, through North Africa, Asia, the western Himalayas, Japan, North America and even south-east Australia.

USDA zone Z6

Description This is a common sight growing wild on the edges of ditches and river banks, but it also makes a super garden plant. It is not technically a reed at all, but has the vague appearance of one. It performs better as a garden plant if sited in deeper water rather than in the shallows or pond margins.

Flowers In summer, small pale green flowers appear on the stems; these flowers are massed in rounded spiky heads or burrs. The female flowers are larger and positioned towards the bases of the branched stalks.

Leaves The leaves are long, green and grass-like; they are deciduous, or semi-deciduous in milder areas.

Cultivation During spring plant young specimens directly into the soil in very large pools, or otherwise into planting baskets. The best position is in full sun, but partial or dappled shade is acceptable. Little on-going care is needed, but dead stems and leaves should be removed in autumn.

Propagation Divide the plants in spring, or sow fresh seeds into mud in submerged pots.

Height Up to 5ft (1.5m) after three years, depending on the depth of water.

Spread Up to 2ft (60cm).

Recommended pond size Medium to large.

Recommended water depth 12in (30cm).

Alternative plants Normally this species is the only form of *Sparganium* to be seen, but it may sometimes be sold under its alternative but less correct name *S. ramosum*.

Tip Try to avoid planting the bur-reed in shallow water where it will soon become a menace.

GOLDEN CLUB (*ORONTIUM AQUATICUM*)

Type Slow-growing perennial. Fairly hardy, tolerating temperatures as low as −5°F (−15°C).

Origin A one-species plant, originally from the Atlantic side of North America.

USDA zone Z7

Description This hardy perennial deserves a position in full view so that visitors can fully appreciate the wonderful golden flower spikes. It's an accommodating plant, and can be grown centrally in a small pool − where it can be truly spectacular − or near the edge of larger ponds.

Flowers *Orontium* is a member of the arum family, but differs in that it does not produce a leafy 'spathe'; in this plant the spathe is reduced to a small, insignificant structure at the base of the long white spikes. These spikes − which appear mid-spring to early summer − each have golden tips like lit candles, and are held just above water level. Small green fruits will develop under the surface of the water when the spikes fade.

Leaves The lance-shaped leaves are deciduous and almost succulent in appearance. They are dark purplish-green beneath and silvery on top. In shallow water the leaves form an erect clump, but can be floating or partly submerged to no detriment elsewhere.

Cultivation Plant young plants in spring, or dormant rhizomes in winter. In ponds use aquatic baskets; ordinary (but deep) garden soil is suitable if *Orontium* is to be grown as a marginal plant. A position in full sun or very light shade is best. Plants are generally trouble-free.

Keep more invasive plants away from *Orontium*. In autumn, remove dead foliage, and apply a mulch of leaf-mould to land-grown plants. It is important not to disturb the plants once they are established.

Propagation Sow ripe seeds in summer, in moist soil or under glass. Rhizomes can be divided in spring; each segment should have a node. Cuttings taken from the roots, in spring, can also be successful.

Height Up to 12in (30cm) above water.
Spread Up to 2ft (60cm).
Recommended pond size Small – up to about 18sq ft (2m²).
Recommended water depth 4–18in (10–45cm).
Tip *Orontiums* seldom require dividing. They should only be disturbed if they are being propagated, or if the baskets in which some may be growing have become crowded.

ABOVE **Golden club (***Orontium aquaticum***) needs to be grown in an open, sunny place for best effect**

LOTUS (*NELUMBO* spp.)

Type Tender perennial tolerating temperatures only down to 34°F (1°C).

Origin Warm Asia to Australia, and eastern North America.

USDA zone Z5 (but for best results treat as for Z9 – overwinter in a frost-free place)

Description There are two species, the hardiest of which is the North American chinkapin (*Nelumbo lutea*). It is the smaller of the two as well, growing to around 5ft (1.5m), with large and showy yellow blossoms. Although not often grown outside in cooler climates, it should produce plenty of typical plate-like leaves, if not many flowers. The sacred lotus (*N. nucifera*) of Asia is a giant of a plant in its original form, but one that has given us a wide range of dwarf cultivars.

Flowers The very showy peony-like lotus flowers open early in the day – often before dawn. Plants can produce a second flush of flowers during late summer or even early autumn, as long as there has been a hot summer.

Leaves Mid-green, round leaves can reach up to 32in (80cm) across in ideal conditions.

ABOVE **The sacred lotus (*Nelumbo nucifera*) is a giant of a plant**

ABOVE **A white form of the sacred lotus**

ABOVE **The pink sacred lotus needs winter protection**

Cultivation Lotus grows best in full sun, in water that often exceeds 59°F (15°C). Overwinter in containers in a frost-free place. Place outside in spring, but only when risk of frosts has passed. Aphids can cause a few problems, but otherwise the plants are generally trouble-free.

Propagation By division; plants are vigorous and division is recommended every two years.

Height Up to 6ft (2m) above water.

Spread Up to 6ft (2m) in all directions.

Recommended pond size Large

Recommended water depth 3–5ft (1–1.5m).

Alternative plants In the case of the sacred lotus, consider the white, pink-edged 'Chawan Basu' or the carmine pink 'Pekinensis Rubra'.

Tip Instead of growing lotuses in the pond try them in a large tub or decorated container at the waterside. When grown in containers like this they can be easily moved indoors during the autumn for overwintering in a frost-free place.

MARE'S TAIL (*HIPPURIS VULGARIS*)

Type Very hardy perennial, tolerating temperatures as low as −4°F (−20°C).

Origin Throughout Europe.

USDA zone Z4

Description I have been asked more times than I care to remember, how to eradicate one of the worst weeds known to humankind − horsetail (*Equisetum vulgare*). The plant we are recommending here bears no relation to that weed, although the name sounds similar (and to add to the confusion there is at least one good equisetum that is sometimes grown as a marginal plant)! *Hippuris vulgaris* is an attractive perennial, and in calm waters in many parts of the world its strongly spreading rhizome forms large colonies. It will not escape notice, even in a small pond.

Flowers Minute, insignificant green flowers appear during summer.

ABOVE **Mare's tail (*Hippuris vulgaris*) has short, narrow leaves spiralling up and along short stems**

Leaves The strength of the plants comes with its foliage. In spirals up the stalks, come many short, narrow, deciduous needle-like leaves.

Cultivation Set young plants or rhizomes into planting baskets during spring. A site in full sun, or lightly shaded, is preferred. Remove dead foliage in the autumn.

Propagation Divide the plants in spring.

Height Up to 12in (30cm) depending on the depth of water in which they are growing.

Spread Up to 18in (45cm) after three years.

Recommended pond size Medium to large.

Recommended water depth Up to 2ft (60cm).

PICKEREL WEED (*PONTADERIA CORDATA*)

Type Hardy. Plants survive the winter, so long as the crowns are below the ice. If grown in soil at the pond edge, protect the crowns in winter with a mulch of bracken or straw.

Origin It is a native of North America, and is called the 'pickerel' weed after the fact that various types of pike hide in amongst its dense growth in the wild.

USDA zone Z3 .

Description A rather ugly name for a glorious plant that is both a hardy herbaceous plant and a shallow or deep-water aquatic.

ABOVE **The white-flowered pickerel weed (*Pontaderia cordata alba*)**

Sited in groups in deeper water, the plants are quite undemanding and come into their own when most other flowers have finished. It is often regarded as the best blue-flowered aquatic plant.

Flowers Tiny, pale blue to purple, massed tightly on cylindrical spikes; mid-summer to early autumn. Not all of the flowers on a spike open at the same time, which can give the individual spike a 'moth-eaten' look. But when grown in sufficient numbers, there is a very splendid mass effect of blue flowers.

Leaves Deciduous, deep green, spear- or heart-shaped leaves on strong stalks rising from the water.

Cultivation Set out *Pontederia* in spring, by planting young plants 12in (30cm) apart, in small isolated groups directly into soil, or in baskets (to limit their spread). They perform well in full sun, but with light shade they have a longer flowering period. Remove dead foliage as it appears.

Propagation In autumn, sow the fresh seeds in submerged pots under glass. Alternatively, divide mature plants in late spring.

Height Up to 30in (75cm) above the waterline.

Spread 18in (45cm) per year.

Recommended pond size To maximize the appreciation of this plant, several should be grown. Therefore the best size of pond is medium to large. Not recommended for water barrels, sinks or the like.

Recommended water depth 4–15in (10–38cm).

Alternative plants The white-flowered form is worth growing; look for *P. cordata alba*. Also, the variety *P. cordata lancifolia* has slimmer leaves, and is a slightly taller plant.

Tip Although *Pontederia* is perfectly acceptable for growing as a marginal plant, it can become invasive and troublesome. Many experienced gardeners prefer to treat them as deeper water aquatics, where they can be grown and 'controlled' in planting baskets.

WATER FRINGE (*NYMPHOIDES PELTATA*)

Type Very hardy, tolerating temperatures as low as −4°F (−20°C).

Origin Europe and Asia, and now naturalized in North America.

USDA zone Z6

Description Very pretty almost buttercup-like flowers are held on stems over attractive leathery leaves, making the whole effect similar to small waterlilies. In fact, some gardeners still refer to this as the 'poor man's waterlily'.

Flowers The yellow blooms appear from mid-summer to early autumn. Each flower is 2in (5cm) across, and each petal has a frilled edge, giving it some distinction.

Leaves Heart-shaped, waxy, deciduous leaves 4in (10cm) across, float on the surface of the water. The leaves are slightly mottled light and dark green, with purple undersides.

Cultivation In spring plant rhizomes or young plants – and unless you have a very large pond, make sure you contain them within planting baskets. This is an invasive plant – be warned! Cut off and remove dead foliage in autumn, before it sinks and pollutes the water. Aphids represent the worst pest; wash them off with small jets of water.

Propagation In spring, lift plants out of the pond and divide them.

Height Up to 4in (10cm) above water.

Spread Up to 2ft (60cm) in each direction after two years.

Recommended pond size Medium to large.

Recommended water depth To 18in (45cm).

Alternative plants Alternative common names for this plant are the fringed waterlily, and the yellow floating heart. Normally only the straight species is seen, but the form 'Bennettii' is becoming more widely available. It produces slightly larger flowers but lacks some of the attractive leaf mottling of the species.

ABOVE **The pretty buttercup flowers of the water fringe (***Nymphoides peltata***)**

WATER HAWTHORN
(*APONOGETON DISTACHYOS*)

Type Hardy. Plants survive the winter, so long as the tubers are below the ice.

Origin Southern tip of Africa. It has not acclimatized to our more temperate flowering seasons, which is why it produces two flushes of flowers per year.

USDA zone Z9

Description The water hawthorn is an excellent plant for deep-water ponds. It is easy to grow and it's very long flowering, especially when grown in shade. It has attractive floating leaves that are more or less evergreen; and the vanilla-like fragrance of the blooms is powerful and lingering. After the main spring crop of blooms, plants generally collapse until late summer, when they often disappear from sight altogether, unless growing in the shade. By mid-autumn, however, they have usually produced a fresh set of leaves and start flowering again, sometimes through to early winter in mild parts.

ABOVE **The water hawthorn (***Aponogeton distachyos***)**

Flowers Late spring and again in autumn, or continuously, if grown in light shade. Soft white with waxy petals and jet black anthers, in forked spikes that almost float on the surface of the water. Strongly fragrant.

Leaves Oval, long and mid-green with brown blotches, floating on the surface of the water. Evergreen in mild parts.

Cultivation Set out water hawthorns in spring, by planting the tubers – or young plants – 18in (45cm) apart, in small isolated groups in baskets, or directly into soil. They perform well in full sun, but with light shade they have a longer flowering period. Remove dead foliage as soon as it appears.

Propagation The freely produced green seeds can be found floating on the surface of the pond during late summer and autumn. Net some ripe seeds, and sow them straight away in containers of water indoors. Alternatively, divide mature plants in late spring.

Height Approx. 4in (10cm) above water.

Spread 2ft (60cm) per year.

Recommended pond size Tiny: even a water barrel could sustain a plant or two.

Recommended water depth 12–36in (30–90cm).

Alternative name Sometimes referred to as the Cape pondweed, and is often seen as *A. distachyus*. A yellow-flowered, more tender species is sometimes available; look for *A. desertorum* (also sold as *A. kraussianum*).

Tip Watch out for snails. They can be very destructive to the leaves, and young plants are particularly at risk.

WATER IRISES

Type Rhizomatous perennials
Origin Worldwide (particularly Japan).
USDA zone Z4–9
Description Stately and colourful, every water garden should have at least one *Iris*. The rhizome is the root of the plant, which should be planted into good-quality topsoil in a planting basket. The rhizome will grow and split into multiple plants, which after a few years can be divided up in the early spring and re-potted into fresh soil and containers.

Flowers Probably the most welcome part of the iris. Nearly all of the water irises are bi-annual flowering, meaning each individual plant only flowers every other year, but when they have grown for a few years and you have a clump of them established you will have flowers every year. There are many forms of flowers: single flowers have three petals and three upright standards (almost petals). The petals have what is known as a signal flash in the centre near the stem, which can be of various colours. Double flowers have six petals – the standards have actually become petals. There are also multi-petalled irises, which are mutations with more than six petals.

Leaves The green leaf part of the plant is called the flag, seen for most of the year. There are many variegated irises which have the flag part coloured by either yellow, cream or white as well as the normal green.

Cultivation Full sun is preferable; light shade is acceptable. Newly bought containerized plants will be growing in a suitable soil, but if you are replanting, use good, clean garden soil from a part of the garden that has not recently been dressed with fertilizer. Remove twigs, weeds, old leaves or anything likely to decay and foul the water. Plant between mid-spring and mid-summer. Little aftercare is needed once plants are established. Remove dead or scrappy leaves when seen. Dead flower heads should be moved before they set seed (unless you want to collect the seed).

Propogation Most varieties will benefit from lifting and dividing every three or four years.

Varieties There are many irises associated with water gardening, and whereas most will only tolerate damp soil conditions, those listed on page 108 are very happy growing in a pond with around 4in (10cm) of water over the soil.

ABOVE **The yellow flag (*Iris pseudacorus*) is the most common of water irises**

The yellow flag (*Iris pseudacorus*), a native plant to Britain, is the most common of water irises, and roots of it will grow most vigorously. It will, within reason, grow in any depth of water, and I have been known to cruelly chop up small sections with leaves and weigh them down in 15in (38cm) of water, with highly successful results. Just remember to divide your plants every couple of years for the best results.

The species is strong growing with large golden flowers and brown signal flashes. It needs a lot of room in which to grow, so should only be planted into a medium to large-size pond.

There are a number of excellent yellow flag varieties. One of the most popular is 'Tangawaray Cream', from New Zealand. It has a lovely pale cream flower with brown signals. 'Wychwood Multifloral' is a seedling from 'Tangawaray Cream', with rich golden flowers but with twice the amount of flowering buds as the original.

'Flore Plena' is a hose-in-hose iris, which means that the flower is constructed from many blooms, each one growing inside another.

The form 'Variegata' has golden flowers with deep yellow and green variegated leaves. The actual variegation is not stable; meaning that the flag reverts to green in late summer, but in the following spring it will once again emerge with wonderful bright yellow and green colourings.

More diminutive are 'Golden Queen', a completely golden iris with no brown signal flashes, and *Iris pseudacorus* 'Bastardii', a cream variety with pale brown signals. For something completely different you could always try 'Ecru', an almost white flower with dark brown signals.

The most important iris for growing in water has to be *I. laevigata*, the Japanese water iris. The three-petalled blooms of straight *I. laevigata* are about 5in (12.5cm) across, and are borne on 2ft (60cm) high stems. The first flowers open in early summer, and are a clear blue-violet with a yellow line down the centre of each petal. If plants are enjoying life in the right conditions, a second flush of flowers may appear in late summer or early autumn. There are many dozens of varieties worth considering, but here are my favourites.

The single white version is called 'Alba'. 'Flore Plena' is a double-flowered version of the species and 'Snowdrift' is a double version of 'Alba'.

The three most stunning forms are 'Weymouth' (single), 'Weymouth Midnight' (double) and 'Regal'. The first two are dark blue with pure white signals, and the third is a deep cyclamen-red flower with white signals.

Iris versicolor, curiously referred to as the American blue flag, actually has a bright green flag with a profusion of small flowers. Its flower stalks are 18–24in (45–60cm) high, the leaves reaching a little higher still. It can come in various colours, the norm being pale blue, through to darker blue, but there are white forms as well as many named varieties. One of these varieties is 'Kermesina', a deep wine red with golden signals. 'Mysterious Monique' has deep red flowers that almost verge to purple. There are also heavily veined varieties: 'Between the Lines' is pure white with pale blue veining throughout, and 'Candy Striper' is a pale cream with medium blue heavy veins.

Louisiana irises are naturally distributed in the warm and wet lands of south Louisiana in the United States. *Iris fulva* and *I.* x *fulvala* are just two varieties, and these are perhaps the best. They each have totally different qualities. The former is a pale brown-red colour, whilst the latter is a much showier plant, with large rich purple flowers and golden signals. Both varieties produce lush green foliage very early in the spring.

WATERLILIES (*NYMPHAEA* spp.)

Type Rhizomatus perennials.
Origin Worldwide.
USDA zone Z4–10
Description Of all the aquatic plants that grow in our ponds, it is the waterlily that epitomizes the subject to many people. To my mind there are few plants – aquatic or land-based – to compare with the pure exotic pleasure that a succession of waterlily flowers can bring.

Fortunately for waterliliophiles like me, there are plenty of varieties to choose from; the sad thing is that the majority of them grow too big for the small ponds that most of us possess today. It is for this reason that in the early 1900s the French hybridist Latour-Marliac, amongst others, devoted himself to the creation of newer and better miniature or dwarf varieties, many of which are classed under the category known as the Pygmaea hybrids. Tragically, he took much of his cross-breeding data with him to his grave, but at least he left us with a fabulous range of small and compact varieties, even if the plant parentage of most of them is not fully known.

The pygmy waterlilies are excellent for sinks, troughs or ponds where the water is no deeper than 12in (30cm). Most will grow contentedly in just 4in (10cm) of water, or even in the deeper marginal shelves of a larger pond.

There are really just two notes of caution when it comes to growing these small and compact varieties. The first concerns the likelihood of the plants freezing in winter: despite being hardy, the plants grow in very shallow water which, in the harshest of winters, can freeze solid. The plants should be provided with sufficient depth to ensure that the rhizomes will remain unfrozen during the coldest spells.

ABOVE **One of the best of the small waterlilies is 'Froebelii' – ideal for growing in a large container**

If this is not possible, they should be protected, either by draining the pool in autumn, and then covering the lily with thick straw, or by lifting the plant in mid-autumn and keeping it in water in a frost-free but light place until planting time again. The second warning is not so serious for the plant, but by ignoring it you could be forfeiting some excellent colour, with resultant substandard plants. Small waterlilies are perfect for growing in contained water features, such as a barrel, tub or sink, but there is a temptation for many of us to fit a small ornamental fountain, or a regular drip-drip feature of some kind.

All waterlilies, of whatever size, dislike moving water around their leaves and stems (which suppresses flowering), and this problem can be exacerbated in a container.

Site Full sun is preferable; plants in water barrels and the like can be left in partial shade where (particularly in summer) the water won't heat up and cool down quite so rapidly.

Soil Newly bought containerized plants will be growing in a suitable soil, but if you are replanting, use good, clean garden soil from a part of the garden that has not recently been dressed with fertilizer. Remove twigs, weeds, old leaves or anything likely to decay and cause pollution in the water.

Planting This should take place between mid-spring and mid-summer. Newly bought containerized plants can be sited straight away, at the appropriate depth for the variety. See below for planting divided offshoots.

Aftercare Little is needed once plants are established. Remove dead or scrappy leaves when seen. Dead flower heads should be removed before they sink.

Division Most varieties will benefit from lifting and dividing every three or four years. This should take place during mid- to late spring. If the flowers rise on their stalks well above the leaves (and they are not the tropical species for which this is normal), or if the leaves are being supported by other leaves and are not laying flat on the surface of the water, it is a reasonably good indication that the plant is congested and in need of dividing. Use garden soil as described above and plant the offshoots in a new aquatic pot, placing gravel or small stones over the compost to prevent fish disturbing it.

Pests and diseases Aphids (blackfly), waterlily beetle, leaf miners, root and rhizome rot and leaf spots are the main problems. As for the water iris information above, chemical controls are not possible, so wash off the pests and be vigilant over the other troubles.

Varieties

'Small' waterlilies

These varieties are ideal for small ponds, or even container water features, with a water depth of 4–12in (10–30cm). When mature, they have a spread of 1–2ft (30–60cm).

'Aurora' (yellow, gradually changing through orange to red, semi-double, yellow stamens, mid-green leaves with mottled and marbled patterns)

'Froebelii' (vivid red, single, yellow stamens, mid-green leaves)

ABOVE **Flowers of 'Paul Hariot' start yellow and turn reddish-orange as they age**

ABOVE **'Comanche' is a compact waterlily offering a great variety of leaf and flower colour**

'Graziella' (coppery-red, single, orange stamens, pale green leaves with purple flecking)
'Johann Pring' (deep pink, single, stamens in two rings – the inner ones pale orange and the outer ones deep pink – dark green leaves)
'Maurice Laydeker' (wine red with white flecks on the outer petals, yellow stamens, single)
'Paul Hariot' (yellow, turning reddish-orange, semi-double, fragrant, yellow stamens, mid-green leaves with purplish flecking)
'Pygmaea Alba' (also sold as *Nymphaea tetragona*; white, single, golden yellow stamens, dark green leaves, dark red beneath, very tiny indeed – almost the only waterlily that can be grown in an aquarium
'Pygmaea Rubis' (wine red, with yellow stamens, single, slightly larger than 'Pygmaea Rubra')
'Pygmaea Rubra' (blood red, orange stamens, single, purple-green leaves with red undersides)

N. x *helvola* (canary yellow, single, orange stamens, olive green leaves, mottled with purple and brown)

'Compact' waterlilies

These are ideal for small ponds, or large contained water features, with a water depth of 1–2ft (30–60cm). They generally have a spread, when mature, of some 2–3ft (60–90cm).
'Albatross' (pure white, single, golden stamens, purplish leaves, gradually turning deep green)
'Brakeleyi Rosea' (fragrant, rose pink fading to flesh and almost white, semi-double, pink stamens, dark green leaves)
'Comanche' (small, deep orange changing to bronze with age, semi-double, orange-red stamens, purple leaves, turning green)
'Ellisiana' (wine red, gradually darkening, single, orange stamens, mid-green leaves)

111

'Firecrest' (pink, semi-double, fragrant, orange stamens with red tips, green-bronze leaves)

'Indiana' (orange-red, ageing to deep red, semi-double, yellow stamens, olive green leaves with darker mottling)

'James Brydon' (one of the most widely seen waterlilies, crimson, semi-double to double, fragrant, red stamens with gold tips, dark purple-green leaves with maroon flecks)

'Laydekeri Fulgens' (bright crimson, single, red stamens, dark green leaves with purple-brown flecks)

'Laydekeri Lilacea' (lilac-pink, single, bright yellow stamens, green leaves with a few brown flecks)

'Laydekeri Purpurata' (wine-red, single, orange stamens, long season of flowering, mid-green leaves with purple flecks)

'Odorata Sulphurea Grandiflora' (yellow, semi-double, yellow stamens, mid-green leaves with brownish markings)

'Robinsoniana' (orange-red, semi-double, yellow stamens, dark green leaves with darker flecking)

'Rose Arey' (rose pink, semi-double, fragrant, orange stamens, purple leaves, gradually turning green)

'Sioux' (yellow, turning orange then rich red, semi-double, yellow stamens, greenish bronze leaves with brown mottling)

'Solfatare' (yellow, turning orange-yellow and then red, single, yellow stamens, dark green leaves with purple blotches and spots)

'Larger' waterlilies

Perhaps the most dramatic of all waterlilies are the larger cultivars which are more suited, by definition, to larger ponds – or even lakes. These require a planting depth of 18–32in (45–80cm), and produce a spread of leaves, when mature, of up to 8ft (2.4m).

'Conqueror' (a good, deep red with white flecks; semi-double, yellow stamens, masses of flowers)

'Escarboucle' (crimson, red stamens, semi-double, fragrant)

'Gladstoniana' (white, golden-yellow stamens, double, fragrant)

'Gonnère' (pink, golden stamens, double)

'Mrs Richmond' (pale pink turning to red, yellow stamens, double)

WILLOW GRASS (*POLYGONUM AMPHIBIUM*)

Type Very hardy, tolerating temperatures as low as −4°F (−20°C).

Origin Throughout the temperate regions of the northern hemisphere.

USDA zone Z5

Description A not-too-often seen plant, but one worth searching for from specialist nurseries. *Polygonums* are infamous for their rapid growth rate (as in the mile-a-minute vine, *Polygonum baldschuanicum*) and potential as weeds (such as the devastating Japanese knotweed, *P. japonicum*). This particular plant is, as the Latin species name suggests, amphibious: it will grow on land and in water. On land it is as rampant as many of its contemporaries. In the water it is altogether more submissive.

Flowers Tiny pinkish or reddish heads appear on spikes from mid-summer to mid-autumn.

Leaves Elongated, oval, mid-green and deciduous. In deepish water they float, whilst in shallow waters the leaves may point upwards, although never vertical.

Cultivation Set out young plants in spring, either in planting baskets, or directly into soil. Aphids and leaf spots can occur; wash off the former with jets of water, and remove leaves affected by the latter. Remove dead foliage at any time.

Propagation Divide the plants in spring, or sow fresh seeds into mud in submerged pots.

Height Up to 6in (15cm) above water.

Spread Up to 2ft (60cm).

Recommended pond size Medium.

Recommended water depth 18in (45cm) – the more shallow the water, the more invasive the plant becomes.

Alternative name This plant may be sold under its older name of *Polygonum amphibium*, and may be referred to by its alternative common name, amphibious bistort.

YELLOW PONDLILY (*NUPHAR LUTEA*)

Type Very hardy, tolerating temperatures as low as −4°F (−20°C).
Origin Eastern United States and the West Indies, across to North Africa and into Eastern Europe and Asia.
USDA zone Z4
Description Compared with waterlilies, species of *Nuphar* are very vigorous and therefore invasive. They are suited only to large, deep ponds or lakes. However, if these are the sort of conditions you can provide, then nuphars are an excellent choice.

Flowers Bright yellow cup-shaped flowers, with an odd cat-like scent (although you can't usually get that close), appear in summer.

Leaves This plant offers two entirely different sorts of leaves: rounded, heart-shaped floating leaves up to 12in (30cm) across, and translucent, feathery, thin leaves under the water.
Cultivation In spring, set out rhizomes or young plants, into baskets (the larger the better). Little attention need be given after this, other than to remove dead foliage or flowers, and to wash off any aphids which dare to make an appearance.
Propagation Divide plants in spring.
Height Up to 6in (15cm) above water.
Spread Up to 6ft (2m) in all directions after two years.
Recommended pond size Large – some experts maintain that this plant should not be recommended for a garden pond because of its invasiveness. It's a good lake plant, however!
Recommended water depth 3–8ft (1–2.5m).
Alternative plants *Nuphar japonica* var. *variegata* and *N. pumila variegata* are much smaller, thriving in a depth of up to 18in (45cm).

ABOVE **The yellow pondlily (*Nuphar lutea*)**

MARGINAL PLANTS

ARROW ARUM (*PELTANDRA UNDULATA*)

Type Semi-evergreen perennial. Hardy, tolerating temperatures down to 5°F (−15°C).
Origin North America.
USDA zone Z5
Description This plant is what we call 'architectural', in that it has good form and structure. Although individual plants are not particularly big, they do look best when planted in large groups. For this reason, they are best suited to larger ponds. Set plants 12in (30cm) apart.
Flowers In early summer, tiny greenish flowers on a short spike enclosed by a conspicuous greenish white spathe, appear. Green berries follow.
Leaves The foliage is bright green, shiny and arrow-shaped. When grown in deeper water, this plant tends to be evergreen.

Cultivation Set plants out during spring in full sun or very light shade. Plant directly into the soil. Remove any faded foliage in late autumn. Some winter protection of plants not under water, by packing straw or bracken around the crowns, would be advantageous.
Propagation Divide the creeping rhizomes in spring.
Height Up to 2ft (60cm).
Spread Up to 18in (45cm).
Recommended pond size Medium to large.
Recommended water depth 0–10in (0–25cm).
Alternative plants This plant may also be found under its old name of *Peltandra virginica*. The white arrow arum (*P. sagittifolia*, or sometimes seen as *P. alba*) has flowers of a purer white, which are followed by red berries.

ABOVE **Arrow arum (***Peltandra undulata***)**

ARROWHEAD (*SAGITTARIA SAGITTIFOLIA*)

Type Hardy. Will survive in temperatures as low as −4°F (−20°C).

Origin UK and Northern Europe.

USDA zone Z7

Description The leaves of this marginal plant are quite distinctive and, when combined with the flowers – particularly on the double form – make this highly desirable.

Flowers From mid- to late summer fairly large spikes of white flowers with black and red centres are produced. The male flowers are at the tops of the spikes and females below.

Leaves Elegant arrow-shaped leaves are held above the water, whilst long ribbons of leaves are produced under water.

Cultivation Grow in full sun or light shade. When growing more than one plant, set them out 9in (23cm) apart. Young plants can be planted directly into the soil. Alternatively, you can plant the tubers by weighing them down and dropping them into the water at the pond's edge. Cut back all growth in the autumn. Aphids can be a problem in summer, so wash them off with jets of water.

Propagation Every second or third year, divide and replant when they get overcrowded. This should be done in spring. Also, seeds can be sown under glass in spring.

Height Up to 2ft (60cm).

Spread Up to 18in (45cm).

Recommended pond size Medium to large.

Recommended water depth 2–12in (5–30cm); the deeper the water, the fewer the flowers.

Alternative plants The old botanical name for this plant is *Sagittaria japonica*, and may still be found under this name in some nurseries. The form *S. latifolia* is similar but less hardy, whilst *S. sagittifolia* 'Flore Pleno' produces exquisite double flowers.

RIGHT **The elegant, arrow-shaped leaves of arrowhead (*Sagittaria sagittifolia*) are very distinctive**

ARUM LILY (*ZANTEDESCHIA AETHIOPICA*)

Type Fairly hardy, to 14°F (–10°C).
Origin South Africa.
USDA zone Z8
Description This plant is perhaps as well known as a pot plant as it is for growing outside at the margins of a pond. It is quite a hardy subject, as long as its crowns are protected in winter by a mulch of straw or bracken – or by at least 6in (15cm) of water. It is a highly variable plant, impossible to say with absolute conviction that it is either hardy or half-hardy, deciduous or semi-evergreen or, when it comes down to it, whether it is best as a marginal or a bog garden plant. One thing is certain, however. When in full bloom, a large clump can be stunning.
Flowers In spring and summer minute flowers congregate on a fragrant yellow spike which comes out from the middle of a large white spathe. Orange or yellow berries will often follow in late summer.
Leaves The large, leathery deep green leaves, shaped like elongated hearts, are very dramatic, giving the garden an 'exotic' feel.
Cultivation Grow in full sun or partial shade, in

ABOVE **The dramatic flower of the arum lily (***Zantedeschia aethiopica***) – a clump in full bloom is stunning**

the damp soil of a bog garden, or at the edge of a pond, in water. Plant in spring.
Propagation Divide plants in spring. Flowers produce many seeds which can be sown the following autumn or spring.
Height Up to 2ft (60cm).
Spread Up to 2ft (60cm).
Recommended pond size Medium.
Recommended water depth 2–12in (5–30cm).
Alternative plants It is sometimes referred to as the calla lily, but not to be confused with the bog arum (*Calla palustris*) – see next entry. The variety *Zantedeschia aethiopica* 'Crowborough' is hardier than the species.

BOG ARUM (*CALLA PALUSTRIS*)

Type Very hardy perennial, tolerating temperatures down to –4°F (–20°C).
Origin Throughout Northern Europe, Siberia and Atlantic North America, but now naturalized in the British Isles.
USDA zone Z4
Description A wonderful herbaceous perennial that is perfectly at home either as a marginal or a shallow water aquatic. It is ideal for concealing the sides of a pond, its stout rhizomes eventually colonizing the shallows and supporting a lush dense carpet of leaves. Arguably, the autumn berries are even more attractive than the flowers.
Flowers These appear in late spring and early summer. They are tiny and yellow-green, studded on a cylindrical spike enclosed by a prominent white funnel-shaped arum-like spathe.
Leaves Broadly heart-shaped, glossy rich green and thick, on long stalks growing from strong creeping rhizomes.
Cultivation Planting in spring, by placing pieces of the rhizomes 9in (23cm) apart directly into wet soil or in baskets. Choose a position in full sun or light shade, in wet soil at the edge of larger ponds, or in shallow water. If planted in baskets, these plants will not spread so rapidly and are easier to keep in check.

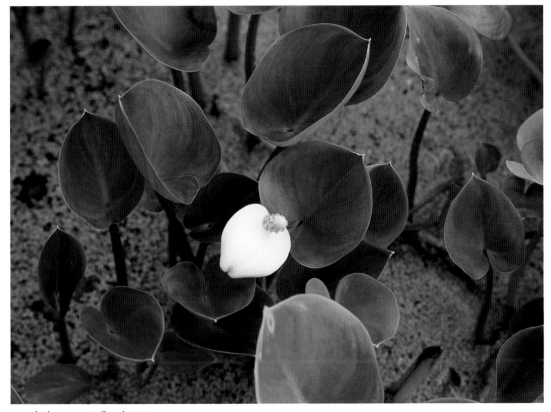

ABOVE **The bog arum (*Calla palustris*)**

Cut down dead foliage in autumn and winter. Keep the plants healthy by dividing the larger clumps every four or five years.

Propagation Divide the rhizomes in spring, then either transplant direct or begin growth in trays of mud under glass and then plant out. The berries – which are poisonous – can be sown when ripe in pots of wet soil.

Height Up to 12in (30cm) when mature.

Spread Up to 12in (30cm) when mature.

Recommended pond size Medium.

Recommended water depth Bog garden, or water to a depth of 8in (20cm).

Related plants *Zantedeschia aethiopica* (formerly known as *Calla aethiopica* and often referred to as the calla lily), is a close relation, and it is an extremely valuable marginal and bog garden plant.

BOG BEAN (*MENYANTHES TRIFOLIATA*)

Type It will tolerate temperatures as low as −4°F (−20°C).

Origin Northern Europe.

USDA zone Z3

Description This plant is best grown as a marginal, but its roots will also creep out into deeper water to grow as an aquatic, where it is less useful. It is not a true 'bean' in the sense that it is in the same family as the runner bean: its leaves resemble those of the broad bean, and that is where any similarity ends.

Flowers White or pale pink star-shaped flowers open between mid-spring and early summer.

Leaves Smooth, shiny and bright green, developing into pointed, oval leaflets.

Cultivation Plant in full sun or part shade. It grows best in a soil that is slightly acidic.

Cut down dead stems in autumn.

Propagation Divide larger clumps, every four or five years. Do this in spring, cutting the creeping rhizomes into several rooted sections. Alternatively, during late summer sow seeds in pots of wet soil.

Height Up to 12in (30cm).

Spread Up to 20in (50cm).

Recommended pond size Medium to large.

Recommended water depth Up to 10in (25cm).

Alternative plants Only this species is available; it is sometimes referred to as the marsh trefoil.

ABOVE Bog bean (*Menyanthes trifoliata*) produces white or pale pink star-shaped flowers

BRASS BUTTONS (*COTULA CORONOPIFOLIA*)

Type Hardy annual or perennial. The severest temperatures tolerated by this plant are in the region of 14°F (–10°C).

Origin South Africa and Southern Asia.

USDA zone Z7

Description This is a pretty little plant, grown either as a short-lived tender perennial (in warmer countries), but more often as an annual plant. Fortunately it usually produces many seeds when the flowers fade, and these help to ensure a further crop of plants for the following year.

Flowers Small, brilliant golden button-shaped blooms appear from late spring to early autumn.

Leaves Fine, shiny and light green; they are also aromatic.

Cultivation Grow in full sun. Plant young plants, or transplant self-sown seedlings in late spring.

Propagation Sow seeds under glass in spring, pricking them out into small pots.

Height Up to 6in (15cm).

Spread Up to 12in (30cm).

Recommended pond size Small.

Recommended water depth 0–4in (0–10cm).

CARDINAL FLOWER (*LOBELIA CARDINALIS*)

Type Will tolerate temperatures only as low as 14°F (–10°C).

Origin North America.

USDA zone Z3

Description This is a red-flowering lobelia, very closely related to the blue annual lobelia so beloved of container gardeners for their showy, overhanging flower cascades. This plant is different in almost every respect, but mainly in that it is hardier, taller and not blue. Although many gardeners are tempted to grow this gem in ordinary garden soil, it really only ever performs at its best when it has its roots under water.

Flowers During late summer and early autumn bright, rich-red flowers will appear in clusters on tall stalks.

Leaves The foliage is shiny, narrow and reddish-green in colour.

Cultivation The best place to plant this lobelia is in full sun or light shade, preferably in shallow water, but it will perform reasonably well in a moist bog garden soil. If you live in a cold part of the country, it would be as well to plant it in a container, and take it to a frost-free greenhouse for winter. Cut down all top growth in autumn and, if sited in a bog garden, cover the crowns with straw or bracken to protect them from the worst of the winter frost. Slugs can be a problem in spring and early summer.

Propagation Sow seeds under glass, or divide plants: both carried out during spring. Alternatively, take soft cuttings of the plants during summer.

Height Up to 3ft (1m).

Spread Up to 12in (30cm).

Recommended pond size Small; even large water containers can house a single plant.

Recommended water depth 2–6in (5–15cm).

Alternative plants *Lobelia fulgens* is larger and more graceful, but slightly less hardy. *Lobelia dortmanna* is a rosette-forming aquatic species, whilst *L. siphilitica* is a very hardy relative with violet-blue flowers. The stunning hybrid 'Queen Victoria' has *L. cardinalis* as one of its parents; it has blood-red leaves and carmine flowers.

ABOVE **The cardinal flower (*Lobelia cardinalis*) throws up spikes of bright red flowers in summer**

COTTON GRASS
(*ERIOPHORUM ANGUSTIFOLIUM*)

Type Very hardy perennial, tolerating temperatures down to −4°F (−20°C).

Origin Throughout the northern hemisphere and into the Arctic regions.

USDA zone Z4

Description Despite its name this is not a true grass, but a species of hardy perennial sedge. It is an elegant native to high-altitude pools, streams, marshes and moorlands with acid soils. Suited to a bog garden, or the margins of a pond, it is extremely slow-growing, and is quite unmistakable in late summer when its seedheads form cotton wool-like tufts. Although cotton grass is not the easiest of plants to grow in low-altitude water gardens, it is certainly one that is well worth trying.

Flowers These appear in early to mid-spring, and are small with bright yellow anthers. They are followed in summer by brown seed pods enclosing tufts of white silky hairs. Allow the flower stems to die down naturally each year.

Leaves Dark green, long, slim and drooping, in clumps.

Cultivation Choose a position in full sun or light shade, in wet, peaty, acid soil at the edge of larger ponds, or in shallow water no deeper than 4in (10cm). Plant during spring 9in (23cm) apart directly into wet soil or in baskets. These are undemanding plants, as long as they have acid soil and water. If growing in the bog garden, as opposed to growing in water, mulch in spring, especially if the soil is likely to dry out.

Feed it with a general fertilizer in spring while young. Keep the plants healthy by dividing the larger clumps every four or five years. If space permits, cotton grass should be planted in bold 'drifts' at the edge of a wildlife pond to create a natural effect.

Propagation By division of larger clumps in spring; either transplanted direct, or started into growth in trays of mud under glass and then planted out. Alternatively sow seeds in wet ericaceous compost under glass in spring.

Height 18–30in (45–75cm) when mature.

Spread Up to 12in (30cm) when mature.

Recommended pond size Medium.

Recommended water depth About 8in (20mm).

Alternative plants The broad-leafed cotton grass (*Eriophorum latifolium*) is slightly larger and tolerates some lime content in the soil and water, but it seems to have a shorter life-span.

FLOWERING RUSH (*BUTOMUS UMBELLATUS*)

Type Will survive temperatures as low as −4°F (−20°C).

Origin Temperate parts of Asia and Europe, including Britain.

USDA zone Z5

Description This not a true rush despite, in some respects, resembling one. It is perfectly at home in the shallow waters of a still pool.

Flowers During mid- to late summer, rose pink blooms are held in rounded heads some 1in (2.5cm) across.

Leaves Narrow, grass-like and green or purplish.

Cultivation Plant in spring in full sun. Cut down all growth in autumn. Sometimes in the summer you may find aphids to be a problem, but they can easily be washed off by jets of water from a hosepipe.

ABOVE **Although not a true rush, the flowering rush (*Butomus umbellatus*) still likes to grow in shallow water**

Propagation Sow seeds under glass in autumn. Divide overgrown clumps every three or four years, in spring.
Height Up to 5ft (1.5m).
Spread Up to 2ft (60cm).
Recommended pond size Medium.
Recommended water depth 1–6in (2.5–15cm).
Alternative plants The white-flowered variety 'Schneeweissen' is excellent.

GREATER SPEARWORT
(*RANUNCULUS LINGUA* 'GRANDIFLORUS')

Type Will survive short periods at –4°F (–20°C).
Origin Throughout Europe and Asia.
USDA zone Z4
Description Most ranunculus species (buttercups and spearworts) can be fairly invasive, but this marginal beauty redeems itself by having very showy flowers.
Flowers Large, 2in (5cm) across, golden yellow and glistening, from mid-spring to early autumn.
Leaves Long, spear-shaped leaves – hence the common name – of bright green, decidedly pinkish when young.
Cultivation Choose a spot in full sun or light shade, and plant in spring either directly into the soil, or into planting baskets for siting on ledges around the pond margins. Remove all of the year's growth at the end of autumn. Mildew may be a problem in late summer and autumn.
Propagation Divide overgrown clumps, probably every three to four years, in spring. Sow seeds in to pots of moist compost in spring, and keep them in a shaded cold frame.
Height Up to 3ft (1m).
Spread Up to 12in (30cm).
Recommended pond size Medium.
Recommended water depth 0–4in (0–10cm).
Alternative plants The lesser spearwort (*Ranunculus flammula*) is less invasive, but not quite as decorative. This plant is well suited for a small pond.

ABOVE **The greater spearwort (***Ranunculus lingua* **'Grandiflorus')**

ABOVE *Houttuynia cordata* 'Chameleon' is an attractive water or bog garden plant, which can be invasive

HOUTTUYNIA CORDATA 'CHAMELEON'

Type Very hardy, tolerating temperatures down to −4°F (−20°C).

Origin Straight *Houttuynia cordata* came originally from the Far East and Asia. 'Chameleon' is a man-made hybrid, introduced within the past 20 years.

USDA zone Z5

Description *Houttuynia cordata* (for which there is no easier-to-pronounce common name), is a vigorous and easily grown semi-evergreen plant for the bog garden or water's edge. It makes attractive ground cover and can become charmingly invasive unless confined in some way. The form 'Chameleon' outsells any of the other forms and its brightly coloured leaves never fail to make a talking point.

Flowers In early summer small, white flowers appear in cone-shaped spikes. Each flower has four petals.

Leaves The real beauty of this plant is in its bold, heart-shaped variegated leaves containing shades of pink, yellow, green, cream and white.

Cultivation Plant during the spring or autumn, directly into the soil at the edge of the pond, or in baskets to restrain root spread. *Houttuynia* prefers a position in partial shade, but will comfortably tolerate full sun or shade. Planting should be into wet soil, or directly into shallow water – but no deeper than 4in (10cm). There is little maintenance required: remove dead or fading foliage when seen, and a general tidy-up in the autumn. Mulch soil-grown plants with compost in the autumn to protect the roots from frost. Aphids and mildew can pose a few problems, but they are not usually serious. Clumps can grow large, so should be divided every four or five years.

Propagation Divide the spreading roots of larger clumps in spring. Gardeners keen to try their propagating skills can sow seed of *Houttuynia* in spring, in a garden frame. Keep the compost moist.

Height Up to 12in (30cm) after three or four years.

Spread Up to 18in (45cm) after three or four years.

Recommended pond size Small to large. The smallest of ponds can only really accommodate single plants.

Recommended water depth 0–4in (0–10cm).

Alternative plants The straight species has mainly green-blue leaves with reddish margins and veining. The form 'Flore Pleno' has double flowers.

MARSH MARIGOLD (*CALTHA PALUSTRIS*)

Type Very hardy, tolerating temperatures as low as –4°F (–20°C).

Origin A native British plant, also found in parts of Northern Europe, America, even as far as the Arctic Circle.

USDA zone Z3

Description The marsh marigold is surely one of the most familiar and loved plants for pondside planting. It is, for want of a better description, a water 'buttercup', with deep golden flowers and large, rounded leaves. Much of the appeal of the plant derives from the neatness of habit: caltha doesn't become straggly and unkempt in the way so many marginals do.

Flowers From mid-spring to early summer, golden yellow, waxy buttercup-like blooms appear, proud of the leaves.

Leaves Glossy, dark green deciduous leaves, more or less rounded, carried on long stalks.

Cultivation Plant in early spring, directly into the soil at the edge of the pond. Caltha prefers a position in full sun or light to medium shade (it is often found naturally in waterlogged woodland soils). Requires little maintenance: remove dead foliage when seen, and a general tidy-up in the autumn. Aphids and mildew can pose a few problems, but they are not usually serious. Clumps can grow large, so should be divided every four or five years.

ABOVE **The marsh marigold (*Caltha palustris*) has deep, buttercup-like flowers and large, rounded leaves**

Propagation Sow fresh seed in late summer or early autumn, in wet soil. You can also divide the spreading roots of larger clumps in spring (or wait until late summer).

Height Up to 32in (80cm).

Spread Up to 20in (50cm).

Recommended pond size Small to medium. The smallest of ponds can only really accommodate single plants. If planting directly into soil under water, there should be a maximum water depth of 6in (15cm).

Recommended water depth 0–6in (0–15cm).

Alternative name Also known as the kingcup (*Caltha palustris*).

Alternative plants Most gardeners tend to grow the single-flowered species. Alternatively there is the tightly double-flowered 'Flore Pleno', which is very free-flowering, or the single-flowered white form, 'Alba' (which is slightly more compact and therefore ideal for smaller ponds). *Caltha leptostyla* is better placed for small ponds. It is smaller than *C. palustris*, with rather dainty star-like, golden-centred white flowers.

Tip For a more impressive display, plant three or more plants together, about 12in (30cm) apart. Massed planting looks so much better than singles, but obviously the size of the pond will dictate whether this is possible.

MARSH ST JOHN'S WORT (*HYPERICUM ELODEOIDES*)

Type Hardy. Will survive –4°F (–20°C) for short periods.

Origin Western Europe.

USDA zone Z7

Description Most hypericums are showy long-lived shrubs, but this small, creeping relative is happiest in mud or shallow water. It is a good plant for concealing the edges of pond liners.

Flowers Small, yellow trumpet flowers appear at the tips of the stems from mid-summer to early autumn.

Leaves These are small, oval and woolly, pale green to green-grey.

Cultivation A sunny spot brings out the best in this plant, but it will tolerate light shade. Plant in groups for best effect. Tidy the plants in autumn, removing dead leaves or flowers.

Propagation Divide large clumps every four or five years, in spring. Take cuttings of soft young growth in summer.

Height Up to 12in (30cm).

Spread Up to 18in (45cm).

Recommended pond size Small ponds but, it has to be said, this plant is perhaps best as a small contribution to a massed planting around a medium-sized pond or larger.

Recommended water depth 0–3in (0–8cm).

Alternative plants This is the only aquatic hypericum, and may be seen under an often-used incorrect name, *H. elodes*.

MUSKS (*MIMULUS* spp.)

Type Will survive temperatures as low as –4°F (–20°C).

Origin North America.

USDA zone Z3–7

Description There are several musk flowers which make excellent plants for pond edges and margins. They really do need room to grow, because they are fairly invasive and have a propensity to self-seed, so larger water gardens make the best homes.

Flowers Usually yellow, orange, red or lavender blue on tall spikes. Close up, the blooms have pronounced lips, rather like snapdragons.

Leaves The foliage is deciduous, small, mid-green and rounded.

Cultivation All of the musks grow best in full sun. Set out young plants, or transplant self-sown seedlings, in spring. Cut back dead or dying stems in the autumn. Mimulus tend to be pest-free, but may sometimes be vulnerable to rots, such as the grey mould fungus.

Propagation Divide overcrowded plants every two or three years, in spring. Take softwood cuttings in summer. Seed of some forms, such as *Mimulus ringens*, can be sown in spring.

Height This varies with the species. Most will reach up to 18in (45cm), but both *M. lewisii* and *M. ringens* will reach double this.

Spread Up to 20in (50cm).

Recommended pond size Medium.

Recommended water depth 0–3in (0–8cm), but 3–6in (8–15cm) in the case of *M. ringens*.

Recommended plants The water musk or yellow musk (*Mimulus luteus*) produces yellow blooms with red blotches during high summer, whilst the blooms of the monkey musk (*M. moschatus*) are all-over yellow. At the same time the lavender musk (*M. ringens*) carries bluish flowers. The great purple monkey flower (*M. lewisii*) carries pink to wine purple flowers from early summer to mid-autumn.

SWEET FLAG (*ACORUS CALAMUS*)

Type Temperatures as low as −4°F (−20°C) will be tolerated.

Origin Asia and North America (although widely naturalized in Europe).

USDA zone Z3

Description This is a popular hardy herbaceous foliage plant which looks like an iris, but is in no way related. Its variegated form is the one most often seen.

Flowers Insignificant, green-brown flowers held on arum-like spikes are carried at the tops of the stems. In warm climates reddish fruits are formed.

Leaves Deciduous, arching, iris-like leaves up to 1in (2.5cm) wide have a very pronounced mid-rib.

Cultivation Plant rhizomes in spring, directly into the soil. Choose a site that is in full sun or very light shade.

Propagation By division in spring.

Height Up to 4ft (1.2m).

Spread Up to 30in (75cm).

Recommended pond size Small to medium.

Recommended water depth 3–10in (8–25cm).

Alternative plants *Acorus calamus* 'Variegatus' produces gold and cream striped leaves, and is

ABOVE **Leaves of the sweet flag (*Acorus calamus*) produce a sweet smell when crushed**

slightly smaller. *A. gramineus* (referred to as the Japanese rush, although the plant is not technically a rush) is about half the size of *A. calamus*, and has almost grass-like leaves.

WATER FORGET-ME-NOT (*MYOSOTIS SCORPIOIDES*)

Type Extremely hardy, tolerating winter temperatures as low as −4°F (−20°C).

Origin Europe and Asia.

USDA zone Z5

Description A common wild plant often found growing on river margins, this is a true and unmistakable forget-me-not, with its jolly blue flowers held on spindly long stems. It is easily grown in most situations, and very reliable. It has creeping rhizomes that are not invasive and will trail into the water, making it an ideal choice for masking pond edges.

Flowers Small, rounded, single flowers of intense azure blue (with a yellow, pink or white eye) appear from mid-spring to mid-summer.

Leaves Small, oval, bright green hairy leaves are carried on long trailing stems. Deciduous.

Cultivation Plant in spring or autumn in moist soil close to the water's edge. Will tolerate a position equally well in full sun and heavy shade (some even say that this plant is the most shade-tolerant of all flowering aquatics). Cut down dead growth in autumn; lift and divide vigorous plants every three years. Watch out for aphids in summer and – just like the garden forget-me-not – mildew towards the end of their annual display. In this case, remove all top growth (leaves and stems) and compost or burn it. Mildew will not kill the plants.

Propagation Divide clumps in spring; separate rooted rhizomes or by transplanting the self-sown seedlings (from species only) in spring.

Height Up to 12in (30cm) above water.

Spread Up to 2ft (60cm); the stems are much longer, but trail down.

Recommended pond size Small to lake-size.

Recommended water depth 0–6in (0–15cm).

Alternative plants There are several varieties worth growing. 'Semperflorens' is a prolific flowerer and has the longest season of all. It has fewer leaves than the others, and is less likely to look straggly. 'Alba' produces white flowers, valuable in the water garden, but is less robust than the blue forms. Other varieties include 'Pinkie', pink, and 'Mermaid', large bright blue flowers over a long season.

Tip Grow some of the white forms in amongst the blue for a breathtaking effect.

ABOVE **The dainty flowers of the water forget-me-not (***Myosotis scorpioides***)**

ABOVE Water mint (*Mentha aquatica*) is useful for attracting bees and other insects to the pond area

WATER MINT (*MENTHA AQUATICA*)

Type Very hardy perennial, tolerating temperatures as low as −4°F (−20°C).

Origin Throughout Europe.

USDA zone Z6

Description A hardy herbaceous perennial, this plant was once one of the most popular of marginal plants for the average garden. Now, mainly because of brighter and better hybridized alternatives, the mint is grown mostly in wildlife ponds. Here, it is an indispensable plant for covering the margins, with its aromatic leaves and flowers that attract bees and other foragers. It is so easy to grow that it can soon become invasive.

Flowers These appear in mid- to late summer. They are characteristic of most mints: tiny, pale mauve and fragrant, in tight, round clusters at the ends of shoots. Prior to flowering, leaf and stem growth can be very rapid, and some control may be desirable. Once the flower shoots start to appear, however, this growth slows down.

Leaves Deciduous. Small, oval, woolly/hairy leaves, dark green turning reddish purple in bright sun. Very heavily scented when crushed.

Cultivation Plant during spring in groups of three or four for impact. Choose a position in full sun, or light to medium shade. If planted in baskets, these plants will not spread so rapidly and are easier to keep in check. Cut down all growth in autumn. Keep the clumps healthy by dividing every three or four years.

Propagation By division in spring; by stem cuttings – exceedingly easy to root – in spring or summer, or by seed, sown in spring.

Height Up to 3ft (1m) when mature.

Spread Up to 30in (75cm) when mature.

Recommended pond size Small.

Recommended water depth 6in (15cm).

Alternative plants *Mentha cervina* is less common, but is slightly daintier; low-growing, it forms leafy clumps with lilac-blue flowers in late summer. Pennyroyal (*M. pulegium*) is closely related; dwarf and sprawling, it also thrives in very wet soil.

BOG GARDEN PLANTS

ARUM ITALICUM 'MARMORATUM'

Type Will survive temperatures as low as 5°F (−15°C)

Origin England, south-east Europe and the Canary Islands.

USDA zone Z6

Description This is a woodland plant and has qualities in triplicate. First, the pretty marbled leaves, which provide the longest period of attraction. Second the flowers – greenish spathes, typical of the aroid family of plants – with their white interiors. And third, the autumn colour provided by the yellow spikes, which are topped with clusters of the brightest blood-orange berries. No self-respecting bog garden would be without this gem.

Flowers In spring creamy white spathes appear, held proud over the ground, followed by stout spikes of rich orange-red berries in autumn.

Leaves Glossy, arrow-shaped and marbled in shades of grey, yellow-green, and green-white.

Cultivation A moist, but not waterlogged, soil is preferred. Plant the tubers approximately 6in (15cm) deep, or as young plants up to the soil mark on the stem base. Little care is required once this arum is established, but it is useful if a handful of general fertilizer is applied around the base of the plant in spring. If slugs eat the autumn berries, control them in the same way as for normal (i.e. non-bog) garden plants: apply pellets, traps or gels, to the soil where the beasts are likely to be most troublesome.

Propagation Divide the plants – carefully, because the stem tissue is soft and easily damaged – in spring or autumn. Collect and sow seed: save the fresh, ripe fruits and wash away every trace of berry flesh; sow in a soil-based compost under glass, and be patient, for germination can take several months.

Height Up to 10in (25cm).

Spread Up to 12in (30cm).

Alternative plants This form may still be found with its old name of *Arum italicum* 'Pictum'. The straight species does not have the attractive leaf marbling.

ASTILBE

Type Temperatures as low as −4°F (−20°C) will be tolerated.

Origin Japan and throughout Asia, also North America.

USDA zone Z5–7

Description These are ubiquitous little plants. I notice them in most gardens I visit – whether or not there are bog gardens – and they are often planted in unsuitably hot, dry and sunny places. But this doesn't really matter, for astilbes are the most accommodating of plants – colourful, easy, dramatic and stately. In all cases they are tough and hardy but, it has to be said, without moisture and shade, they can fall well short of their display potential.

Flowers Flowering generally begins in early summer and the attractive plume-like heads of tiny flowers, which last for several weeks, ensure that the astilbe owner has a good return on investment. The rusty-brown seedheads produced in late summer and autumn are almost as effective as the flower spikes.

Leaves From mid-spring onwards the leaves appear and develop, all deeply cut and often purplish or bronzy green.

Cultivation Moisture is more important than shade, and astilbes should not be allowed to dry out. Rich soil – plenty of compost, with an annual mulch when dormant – will go a long way to making good any moisture deficiency. Some shelter from strong winds will also be helpful, as this prolongs the flowering period. Given reasonably constant moisture, an annual mulch and, perhaps, a little dappled shade, plants can be left for years.

Propagation They can be divided, without much difficulty, when they're old and dormant.

ABOVE *Astilbe x* 'Bressingham Beauty'

ABOVE *Astilbe x arendsii* 'Fanal'

Height Astilbes vary in height from 4in to 6ft (10cm to 2m), and even the tallest need no staking.

Spread Up to 2ft (60cm).

Varieties The gardener cannot complain about the lack of choice. The hybrids borne out of *Astilbe* x *arendsii* are the most commonly seen, and these generally will produce plumes up to 3ft (1m) in height. One of my favourites is the bright pink 'Bressingham Beauty', an old stager but nevertheless still one of the best.

The variety 'Fire' is often found under its German name 'Feuer' and, not surprisingly, produces a brilliant red flower head.

For possibly the purest white arendsii hybrid, go for 'White Queen', but others to be recommended include: 'Amethyst', lilac purple; 'Hyazinth', sugar pink; 'Irrlicht', white with dark leaves; 'Venus', pale pink and slightly taller; 'Federsee', intense salmon pink, and 'Fanal', rich orange-red.

The species *A. simplicifolia* has added its quota to the range of hybrids. The straight type is pretty, with graceful pink spikes 15in (38cm) tall, but the variety 'Atrorosea' is superb, carrying sheaves of tiny bright pink flowers for a long time. There is white in this range, and a charming dark-leafed pink variety only 9in (23cm) high called 'Bronce Elegans'. For this, and the salmon 'Dunkellachs', shade as well as a humus-rich soil is needed.

Happily, 'Sprite' is more adaptable. This has dark leaves which look most effective with the sprays carrying masses of tiny flowers of pale

ABOVE **The salmon pink blooms of** *Astilbe x arendsii* **'Bumalda'**

shell pink. 'Sprite' will grow to 12in (30cm), and the same across, making it ideal for the front of the border.

There are a couple of varieties from the species *A. japonica* that are worth mentioning, both growing to about 2ft (60cm). The white 'Deutschland' is regularly used for forcing as pot plants, and 'Etna' carries beautiful rich red plumes above mounded foliage.

'Professor van der Weilen' is a hybrid from the Japanese species *A. thunbergii*. It is a graceful plant, with handsome leaves, topped by arching sprays of creamy white flowers. It is a little taller – at 4ft (1.2m) – and flowers in mid-summer, a bit later than most.

Where height variations are important there should be room for such beauties as *A.chinensis tacquetii* 'Superba'. This grows to a stately 5ft (1.5m) with dark outspanning foliage and noble spikes of bright rosy purple flowers over a lengthy period. 'Intermezzo' is mid-pink and very floriferous.

And finally, there is *A. chinensis pumila*. This has a creeping habit of fresh, crispy leaves, close to the ground. It has stumpy 12in (30cm) spikes of lilac-rose colour, and is less fussy about moisture than most.

Tip The roots of astilbes are very thirsty and, in a hot drought, watering overhead can be ineffective. Take several large tins – paint pots or large soup tins are perfect – and sink them between the plants so that the rims come to about an inch below the soil surface. It will be easiest to do this during late winter or early spring, when the plants are dormant. During hot summer weather you will be able to fill the tin with water once a day, and moisture will percolate through. One tin will be sufficient for three plants.

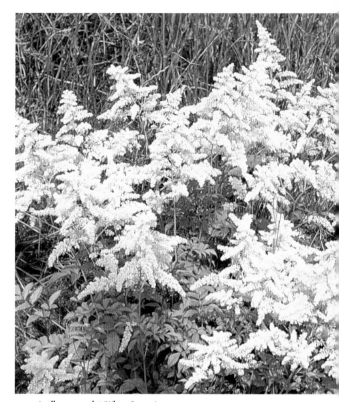

ABOVE *Astilbe x arendsii* **'White Queen'**

RIGHT *Astilbe chinensis* **'Intermezzo'**

BUGLE (*AJUGA REPTANS*)

Type Will survive temperatures as low as −4°F (−20°C).

Origin Northern Europe.

USDA zone Z6

Description This shade-loving ground-cover plant thrives when growing under trees and shrubs, as long as the soil is moderately moist all the time. The greatest irony with ajuga is that the dark-coloured leaves are not seen at their best when the plant is growing in a shady place. Yet if you transfer the plant to a sunnier spot, in order to enjoy its foliage, it sits and sulks and never performs its best. If this is a mystery, however, it is no greater than the one surrounding its common name. Why is it called a bugle? I'm not certain anyone knows.

Flowers Short spikes of small, lipped, purple flowers appear in spring.

Leaves Rounded leaves of deep green with reddish-purple tints.

Cultivation Give the plants a little general fertilizer in spring, followed by a mulch. Trim the plant back, in autumn, if you need to restrict its spread. Mildew can be a problem later in the season, but this is not life threatening.

Propagation By division in spring.

Height Up to 6in (15cm).

Spread Up to 3ft (1m).

Alternative plants The form 'Alba' has whitish flowers, 'Atropurpurea', purple, with deep purple-bronze leaves; 'Variegata' has deep green leaves with cream margins, whilst 'Burgundy Glow' has claret-coloured leaves. The form 'Multicolor' (which may also be found under the names 'Rainbow' and 'Tricolor') has blue flowers and dark bronze leaves splattered with blotches of pink, red and cream.

ABOVE **The leaves of bugle (*Ajuga reptans*) will trail over a low wall. This is the cultivar 'Burgandy Glow'**

DAY LILIES (*HEMEROCALLIS* spp.)

Type Very hardy, surviving temperatures as low as −4°F (−20°C).

Origin Many day lilies originated in Eastern Europe and Asia, but some have been grown in the UK since the 16th century. To the average gardener, however, it is the many dozens of modern hybrid forms which offer most range of colour and habit.

USDA zone Z4–6

Description The individual flowers of the day lily do indeed last just one day. They can be grown in any part of the garden, but they perform best in reasonably moist soil, which means that they make luxuriant additions to any bog garden. They look fabulous next to a pond, too, and an almost surreal appearance can be achieved when their arching stems are reflected in the clear water of a still pool.

ABOVE *Hemerocallis* 'Pink Damask' can be seen in a variety of colour ranges, from pink to salmon

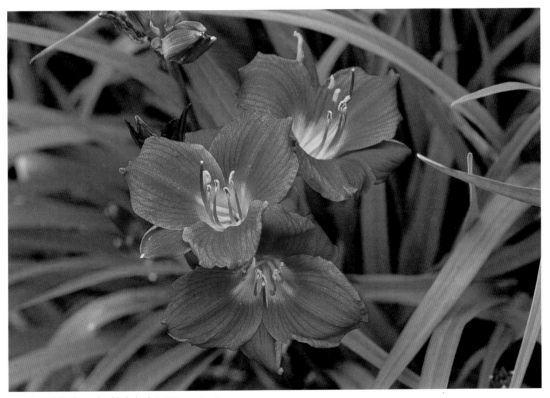

ABOVE One of the finest day lily hybrids is 'Crimson Icon'

ABOVE *Hemerocallis* 'Stella d'Oro'

ABOVE **The arching early spring foliage of** *Hemerocallis*

ABOVE *Hemerocallis* 'Berlin Yellow'

Day lilies have come in for a great deal of attention in recent years from hybridists in Europe and North America. Growers in the early 1900s, such as George Yeld and Amos Perry, raised many beautiful varieties, but only a handful of these are still available commercially.

However, because of the popularity of these plants, dozens of other hybridists were encouraged to 'have a go', and several thousand named forms have been created. Many have disappeared from cultivation because they were surpassed in excellence by newer forms. Even so, there are well over 300

134

varieties available to the gardener today (especially in the USA, where certain sections of the gardening community regard them as cult plants).

Flowers The individual trumpet-shaped flowers are not particularly attractive in their own right, particularly when they are a day old and are on the wane. The real beauty is when you see a mass of flowers. The varieties that produce flowers of a single colour, with the colour repeated on the outside of the trumpet, are far more effective in a border than those that have their main colour concentrated inside the trumpet, as it can then only be seen if the flower is looked at end on. But beware of some of the 'red' varieties – there is no true scarlet or carmine yet available; they can also look scrappy en masse and add nothing to the overall effect of the border. Nearly all the yellow varieties have the bonus of being scented, whereas most of the other varieties are not.

Leaves The arching, rushy leaves are a feature in their own right in spring: they are the brightest of greens, and grow almost an inch a day. At flowering time the leaves complement the trumpet flowers, which come on smooth stems 18–36in (45–90cm) tall.

Cultivation They can be planted at any time from early autumn to mid-spring. Soil should be enriched in advance and, when the plant is fully established, some general fertilizer and mulching in spring will encourage fine flowers. The best site is in full sun or light shade (heavy shade depresses flower production). Most soils are tolerated, but plants are best in fairly rich, loamy soil. Cut dead flower stalks back to the base as soon as the last flowers on them have faded. Cut away all foliage, right back to soil level, in the autumn or else it will turn to an untidy mess over winter.

Propagation Divide plants in autumn or spring. I spade through a clump in situ – either to reduce its size or to obtain sections to plant elsewhere.

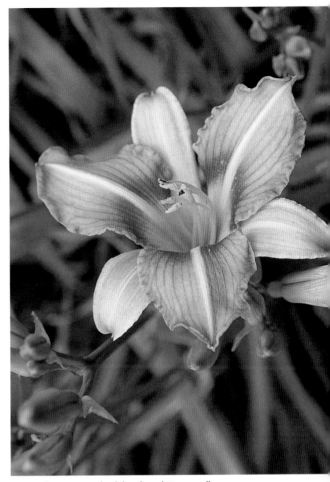

ABOVE **'Stoke Poges' is a brightly coloured** *Hemerocallis*

Such a fearless course has never resulted in harm to the plants and is certainly easier than digging up a big plant and then dividing it.

Height Up to 3ft (1m).

Spread Up to 3ft (1m).

Hybrids The following are some of the best garden hybrids: 'Orangeman', first bred in 1906, is a gorgeous deep orange. 'Hyperion' was introduced nearly 50 years ago, and is still in demand for its clear colour and large yellow flowers. A newer and outstanding yellow is 'Lark Song'. Then there is 'Black Magic', which is a deep ruby mahogany; 'Contessa', light orange; and 'Bonanza', soft yellow but very dwarf.

This matches well with the deeper-coloured 'Golden Chimes', which is also dwarf; and 'Crimson Icon', which has crimson petals with a lemon yellow centre.

'Dubloon' (sometimes sold as 'Golden Orchid') is superb, rich gold and growing to 3ft (1m). 'Nigrette' is mahogany purple; 'Pink Damask' ranges from true pink to salmon; 'Primrose Mascott', pale lemon; 'Stafford', bronzy red; 'Anzac', rich red; 'Luxury Lace', lavender; and 'Stella d'Oro', dwarf yellow.

'Corky' is one of the latest to flower. It has much smaller and more refined blooms than most other hybrids. The petals are yellow with a broad bronze stripe down the reverse of each.

'Catherine Woodberry', pink with yellow markings, is another excellent form, as are 'Hornby Castle', dull brick-red; 'Morocco Red', maroon with a yellow throat; 'Pink Prelude', pink; 'Little Wine Cup', burgundy red with a yellow throat; 'Cream Drop', with exquisite small, creamy yellow flowers; 'Buzz Bomb', deep velvety red; 'Chartreuse Magic', canary yellow and green; 'Berlin Yellow', good, solid yellow all over and 'Stoke Poges', pink with orange markings.

There are only a handful of double-flowered varieties, and they don't generally add that much to the range. Arguably the best double is *H. fulva* 'Kwanso Flora-Plena', which has reddish orange flowers.

Recommended varieties

Although there are several species available, these tend to be found only in specialists' gardens. The earliest show colour in late spring, as in the case of the early and dwarf species *H. dumortierii*, which has yellow flowers lasting for several weeks. *H. citrina* and *H. lilioasphodelus* are charming, fragrant yellow species for late spring and early summer. *H. multiflora*, produces lovely, pale orange-yellow flowers in great profusion from mid-summer to mid-autumn.

FERNS

Type They vary, tolerating temperatures from 14°F (−10°C) down to −4°F (−20°C).
Origin Worldwide.
USDA zone Z2–4
Description Few plants suggest the prehistoric age quite like the fern and these shade-loving plants have been around since the dinosaur, which means that they are sturdy, durable and hardy. More often than not they grow in damp places although, it has to be said, a dank atmosphere is as important to them as a wet soil. Indeed, it is quite a common occurrence for the crown and roots of outdoor ferns to rot in very wet soil.
Flowers Ferns do not flower and produce seeds in the conventional sense − they reproduce by means of spores, which are often seen as small brownish pustules on the undersides of the fronds.
Fronds Ferns make up for the lack of colour by boasting a wide variety of frond shapes and sizes, most in varying shades of green.
Cultivation In spring plant single, specimen plants in full sun, or light to moderate shade. The ideal soil is moist and acid, with plenty of humus. Mulch with garden compost after planting, and annually in spring, and feed with a general fertilizer at the same time. With deciduous ferns it is advisable to protect the emerging young fertile fronds in spring by leaving the dead fronds in place at the end of autumn. Cut these back in spring when the worst of the weather is past, and the new shoots are starting to emerge.
Propagation Divide congested clumps in spring but beware − this is not always an easy job, particularly with the larger forms like *Osmunda*. Chopping off a small portion may be all that is possible. Another way of increasing stock of the fern is to surface-sow ripe spores under glass in autumn or spring. But again, beware! Although ferns produce liberal quantities of spores, many have a very short life, their viability being little more than a few days after ripening.

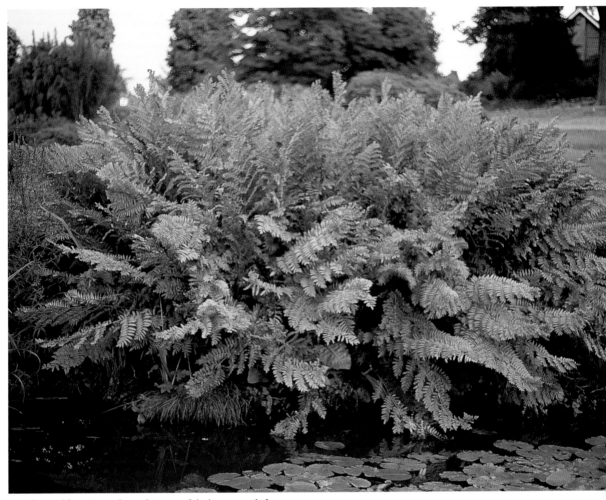

ABOVE **The royal fern (*Osmunda regalis*) is one of the best waterside ferns**

Recommended species The royal fern (*Osmunda regalis*) is generally considered to be the best fern for pondside or bog garden planting and it is, arguably, the most impressive of all the hardy deciduous ferns. It was once common in the wild wet fens and marsh banks of Europe, but is now most often seen in gardens. It is a highly desirable plant for large pond and streamside situations, and is very vigorous and spreading, although some of the cultivated forms are less demanding of space. The lime green, prettily divided fronds first appear as copper-tinted crooked shoots in spring, and finally turn yellow and bronze in autumn. Smaller, stiffer, spore-bearing fronds arise from the centre of the plant.

Closely related forms include *O. regalis* 'Purpurascens', which has purple-green stems and fronds, and markedly pink-brown young shoots; the crested royal fern, 'Cristata', and 'Undulata' are smaller and have attractively tasselled foliage.

The interrupted fern, *O. claytoniana*, derives its common name from the spores that are borne around the stalk in a part of the frond which is devoid of leaflets. Leaflets above and below this

137

ABOVE **The sensitive fern (*Onoclea sensibilis*) is 'sensitive' to autumn frosts**

spore area develop quite normally, giving the entire frond the appearance of having been interrupted.

Much smaller yet just as invasive is the plant variously known as the ostrich plume or shuttlecock fern (*Matteuccia struthiopteris*). It has a reputation for being a bit of a thug, as it will grow and multiply if it is happy with its soil and growing environment. However, if you have the space it is a 'must'. It's deciduous, but come spring the new fronds unfurl in gold and bronze tints before becoming the freshest of lime greens.

The sensitive fern (*Onoclea sensibilis*) is a lovely fern reaching about 2ft (60cm) high. The triangular fronds have a pinkish tinge when they first open. Sadly, these fronds are most sensitive – hence its common name – to autumn frosts. Although the plant is extremely hardy, the fronds are not. Even so, I wouldn't be without this plant.

GIANT PRICKLY RHUBARB (*GUNNERA MANICATA*)

Type Fairly hardy, tolerating temperatures down to 5°F (–15°C).

Origin South America, specifically the lower slopes of the Andes.

USDA zone Z7

Description It is almost compulsory for those of us with big water gardens to grow *Gunnera*. It is our largest hardy herbaceous plant, and many call it the giant, or prickly rhubarb, because of the supposed similarity of its leaves; in truth the two plants are not even related. Close inspection will show that the plants are very different and, anyway, the *Gunnera* is much more spectacular. As long as there is sufficient space, even in a small garden, *Gunnera* will help to create an exotic feel. Its oversized leaves afford shelter for all manner of garden wildlife –

ABOVE **The giant prickly rhubarb (*Gunnera manicata*) is the grandest of bog garden plants**

even waterfowl. Excellent plant combinations can be achieved with *Gunnera* and ornamental grasses such as *Miscanthus*.

Flowers Conical clusters of small greenish-red flowers appear in late spring and early summer. These flower spikes can themselves reach 5ft (1.5m) in height. Rust-brown seed pods follow.

Leaves The vast jagged and indented leaves are the main reason for growing *Gunnera*. Individual leaves on some mature plants can reach to 6ft (2m) in diameter. These are carried on thick stems with nasty spikes on the biggest.

Cultivation Choose a position in full sun or medium shade, at the edge of larger ponds. Plant during spring. They are undemanding plants, as long as they have some shelter from the coldest of winds and the latest of frosts. Cut back the dry leaves in autumn; in colder areas, it is advisable to give the plants a protective mulch with straw, sacking or horticultural fleece.

ABOVE **A close-up of the complex flower spike of** *Gunnera manicata*

Gunnera tolerate most soils, but prefer deep, fertile soils with high moisture content. Feed with a general fertilizer in spring.

Propagation By division of larger clumps in spring, or by seeds sown fresh in the autumn. Choose a loam-based compost and store the growing seed in a sheltered cold frame.

Height Up to 10ft (3m) when four years old.

Spread Up to 16ft (5m) when four years old.

Alternative plants The giant Chilean rhubarb (*Gunnera tinctoria*) is slightly smaller and slightly hardier. Leaves on mature plants are just 3ft (1m) wide, and the overall height is 6ft (2m). Alternatively, opt for the dwarf, carpet-creeping gunnera, *G. magellanica*. It has bright green 'crinkled' leaves, and plants barely reach 4in (10cm) in height, with a spread of 3ft (1m).

ABOVE **Some leaves of** *Gunnera* **can reach 6ft (2m) in diameter**

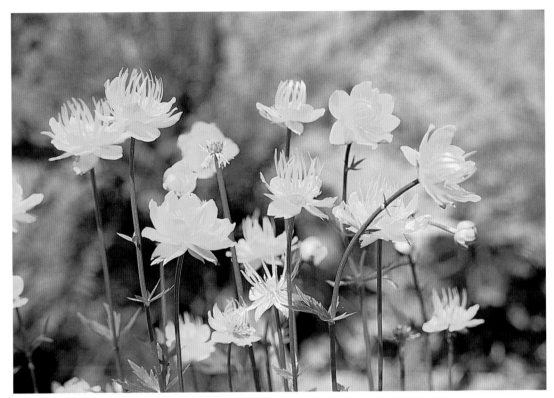

ABOVE *Trollius chinensis* 'Golden Queen'

GLOBE FLOWER (*TROLLIUS EUROPAEUS*)

Type Will survive temperatures as low as −4°F (−20°C).

Origin Europe.

USDA zone Z5

Description The globe flower has been attacked heavily by plant breeders over the years, and now there are many varieties which, in some respects, lack some of the charm of the original plant. It is a non-invasive hardy herbaceous perennial which looks most effective when grown in groups – as it would be in the wild.

Flowers Bright yellow spherical flowers are carried on wiry stems during late spring and early summer.

Leaves Fern-like leaves, heavily divided and deep green.

Cultivation This plant likes a position in full sun or light shade, and looks good when growing amongst rocks. Plant in spring or autumn, preferably in groups. Mulch with well-rotted compost in the spring. During the flowering season, make sure you remove the faded flowers as quickly as possible, as this encourages more flowers to bloom.

Propagation Divide plants in spring or autumn (overgrown clumps will need dividing every three or four years anyway). Alternatively, sow seeds under glass in spring.

Height Up to 30in (75cm).

Spread Up to 18in (45cm).

Alternative plants More fiery colours than the yellow species are available from the numerous hybrids. Try the following: *Trollius* x *cultorum* 'Alabaster', cream; 'Canary Bird', orange; 'Feuertroll' (also seen as 'Fireglobe'), deep orange; *Trollius chinensis* 'Golden Queen', orange-yellow.

GOAT'S BEARD (*ARUNCUS DIOICUS*)

Type Very hardy, tolerating temperatures down to −4°F (−20°C).

Origin The mountain woods and shady stream-sides of Central Europe, China, Japan and North America.

USDA zone Z7

Description The elegant leaves, majestic flowers and tall stems make this plant an erect and stately star of the bog garden. The normal species needs plenty of room in which to spread, so if space is not a problem, this plant is a must.

Flowers In early and mid-summer, tiny, cream-white blooms appear on large fluffy flower heads. Arguably, *Aruncus* is just as attractive in the early flower stage – when the stems are delicately lined with tiny round buds – as it is when the great creamy plumes have all exploded into foaming flowers.

Leaves Numerous deeply serrated leaflets of fresh green are arranged on long stems.

Cultivation Plant during the spring or autumn, directly into rich, moist and peaty soil. *Aruncus* prefers a position in light or moderate shade. There is little maintenance required: like other perennials, cut back the dead top-growth in late autumn, and take this opportunity for a general tidy-up. Mulch soil-grown plants with compost in the spring or autumn. Provide a few handfuls of general fertilizer in the spring. *Aruncus* has very stiff stems, so does not need staking. Clumps can grow large, so should be divided every three or four years. *Aruncus* is virtually pest and disease free.

Propagation Divide the spreading roots of

ABOVE **The elegant leaves and flowers of goat's beard (*Aruncus dioicus*) need plenty of room in which to grow**

larger clumps in spring or autumn. Or sow seeds in summer or early autumn in a humus-rich, soil-based compost. Provide protection, such as that supplied by a cold frame or unheated greenhouse.

Height Up to 6ft (2m).

Spread Up to 4ft (1.2m).

Alternative plants The old name for this plant is *Aruncus sylvester*, and some nurseries may still be selling it under this name. The normal species is the best, but for smaller gardens there is the variety 'Kneiffii', which grows to about half the size. The leaves of this smaller form look as though they have been eaten to the veins by some creature, but this makes them very attractively lacy.

GRASSES AS ORNAMENTAL FEATURES

Type Varies depending on the species, but most will survive temperatures as low as 5°F (–15°C), some even lower.

Origin Worldwide.

USDA zone Z5–8

Description Only a few years ago, no more than a handful of decorative, ornamental grasses would have been listed in plant catalogues. Now they are very fashionable, and there is a bewildering array of species and varieties, from the architectural pampas grass to the clump-forming smaller forms, like *Festuca*. Not all grasses like a really wet or waterlogged soil – moist but free-draining seems to be the motto.

Cultivation Plant in spring, in full sun or light shade. Mulch in autumn and spring and give a balanced general fertilizer in spring. Leave the top-growth over winter, and reduce it in early spring before new growth commences. Divide the clumps every four or five years to keep the plant healthy.

Propagation By division in autumn or spring.

Recommended species One grass which revels in boggy conditions is the reed sweet grass (*Glyceria maxima* var. *variegata*), which is

ABOVE *Schoenoplectus lacustris* 'Albescens'

vigorous and can be invasive – growing in a sunken container will alleviate this problem. Its young foliage has a pinkish hue which then becomes boldly variegated with white and yellow as it ages.

The cream variegated grasses are particularly attractive. One which never fails to impress is the golden hakone grass (*Hakonechloa macra* 'Alboaurea') with its brilliant yellow-striped blades. It is a low grower, not exceeding 12in (30cm), and forms a dense mat which in time becomes a sizeable clump.

One of the brightest of grasses is the golden wood millet (*Milium effusum* 'Aureum'). It is most spectacular in spring when the growths are young.

ABOVE *Carex elata* 'Aurea' may also be found under the name 'Bowles' Golden'

It has a loose-growing, tufted habit, and will not get taller than 2ft (60cm). It can also self-seed, but it will not become a nuisance.

Another fabulous variety is Bowles' Golden sedge (*Carex elata* 'Aurea'). Its brown, fairly uninspiring flowers appear in mid-spring. But after these have faded, the plant throws up long, arching leaves of the strongest yellow. A very narrow green margin is present on each leaf making the plant most spectacular. The colour deepens until mid-summer, when it fades gradually to green.

A rush which has grass-like properties, *Schoenoplectus lacustris*, is seen in many natural and cultivated gardens, but is often disregarded because it appears 'normal', with no apparent outstanding qualities. However, on closer inspection, its foliage is variegated and in its own way quite striking. Look for the varieties 'Albescens' with longitudinal green and white stripes, or 'Zebrinus' with horizontal cream stripes on a background of green.

The *Pennisetums* are grasses best grown in a sunny position, otherwise they will need some protection. One of the best clump-formers is *Pennisetum orientale* which has light green, rather hairy leaves. It is grown mainly for its flower spikes which rise 18in (45cm) high.

These have a bottle-brush shape, initially in a mauve-grey colour, slowly changing to a golden brown.

The *Festucas* are generally low-growing, ideal subjects for the front of a border. They require light, well-drained soil, and for best effect should be planted into small groups. 'Golden Toupee' forms a neat, tight cushion with fine, almost needle-like leaves which, like the *Milium*, is best in spring when it is an almost iridescent yellow. As it ages, the colour turns to lime green. Among the most popular *Festucas* are those with blue-grey leaves, such as the excellent 'Elijah Blue'.

Meadow foxtail grass (*Alopecurus pratensis* 'Aureovariegatus') is worth growing in a sunny spot, but don't be misled by the common name: it makes a fabulous plant for the bog garden. In early summer it produces the most delightful, soft, tubular flower head with a slight purple hue. The leaves have some of the most golden stripes of any grass.

Lastly, if you want something with a hot colour, choose the Japanese blood grass (*Imperata cylindrica* 'Rubra'). Its young leaves are as red as you can get.

IRISES

Type Hardy rhizomatous perennials.
Origin Worldwide.
USDA zone Z4–9
Description Several species of iris will flourish in the damp soil of a bog garden, but only two are really popular and neither of them likes over-wet soil in winter.

Iris ensata (which used to be known, and is still sometimes sold as, *I. kaempferi*) is the delightful Japanese clematis iris, so-called because the blooms flatten out to resemble the star-shaped blooms of clematis. It grows to a height of 24–30in (60–75cm), and flowers during late spring and early summer. The downside is that an acid soil is essential. It has broad leaves and large, flattened flowers.

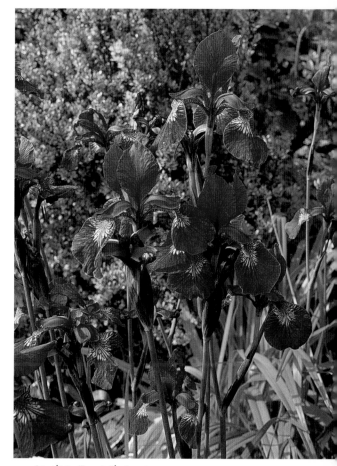
ABOVE *Iris sibirica* **'Perry's Blue'**

ABOVE *Iris ensata* **'Barr Purple East'**

145

ABOVE *Iris sibirica* 'Silver Edge'

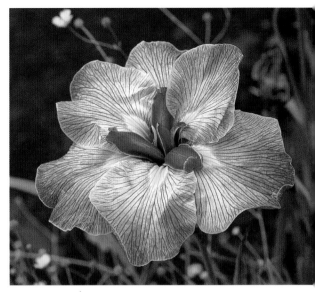

ABOVE *Iris ensata* 'Flying Tiger'

ABOVE *Iris ensata* var. *spontanea* produces deep purple flowers, each with a fetching gold streak

I. ensata can be grown from seed; there may be some variation of colour, but all should be good.

There are, literally, hundreds of varieties of ensata. Three of the best are 'Flying Tiger' (pale blue with yellow inside the petals), 'Barr Purple East' (which is deep purple) and *I. ensata* var. *spontanea* (purple with a golden streak inside the petals).

Meanwhile, the Siberian iris, *I. sibirica*, is an easier plant to grow. I have two clumps of 'Perry's Blue', untouched for about nine years, growing on quite a limy soil. They could do with a bit of thinning once the flowers have finished; the centres of ageing clumps tend to become 'bald' with a ring of growth progressively moving outwards each year.

At flowering time the first of two buds from each stem opens and does its thing. The second bud opens as the first fades. At the end of the flowering season the highly glossy green seed pods are formed, and these have an attraction all of their own; remove them in the autumn to keep the clump tidy.

The leaves of *I. sibirica* are grass-like, and the flowers smaller than most other water irises, but there are many excellent varieties, and several good dwarf forms, including 'Flight of Butterflies' (dark blue veined purple) and 'Silver Edge' (deep blue with white edges to the petals).

If the ground remains very wet in winter, try growing *I. orientalis*, formerly known as *I. ochroleuca*. It is easy to grow, and even grows in salty marshes in its wild habitat in the Middle East. It usually grows to 3ft (1m), producing white and egg-yolk yellow flowers.

Propagation To propagate all of the irises mentioned here, especially if the desire is to keep the offspring true to their parent, dividing the clumps into individual plants after flowering is the only method. In most cases, the sooner this is done after the flowers fade, the better, but with *I. ensata* it is best to wait until autumn, before the leaves have finally died down.

LADY'S MANTLE (*ALCHEMILLA MOLLIS*)

Type Extremely hardy, tolerating temperatures down to −4°F (−20°C) and probably lower.
Origin Fairly widespread, from Europe, to Asia, Labrador and even Greenland.
USDA zone Z4
Description This is one of the most familiar of border plants, beloved of flower arrangers for the soft, wispy green flowers and thick, uniquely serrated leaves. For the gardener it is a fine, architectural hardy herbaceous perennial, and it is a must for any bog garden. Although there are around 30 species of alchemilla, this is the form that is best for the bog garden.
Flowers Tiny, soft yellow-green flowers are held in umbrella-like clusters throughout summer.
Leaves Large, many-lobed leaves which have fine serrations. The attractive foliage appears to be both waxy and downy at the same time.

ABOVE **Lady's mantle (*Alchemilla mollis*) is an excellent border plant and is often used in flower arrangements**

It's a cliché to eulogize over the apparent compulsion for droplets of rainwater and dew to collect in the bowls of the leaves, but they do make this plant a little special.

Cultivation Ideally, this plant needs dappled shade, as direct sunlight for long periods during summer days can turn some of the leaves crispy. Mulch around the base of the plant in spring and/or autumn, and it is advisable to throw a handful of general fertilizer around the base of the plant in spring. Remove the faded flower heads and cut all old growth down to ground level at the end of autumn.

Propagation By division in spring or autumn. Or by seed sown in autumn. This plant will readily self-sow and come up in some unusual places in the garden; it is not, however, usually regarded as a nuisance, as the young seedlings can be most welcome.

Height Up to 20in (50cm).
Spread Up to 20in (50cm).

MARSH GENTIAN (GENTIANA PNEUMONANTHE)

Type Hardy. It will survive temperatures down to −4°F (−20°C).
Origin Native throughout the northern hemisphere.
USDA zone Z4
Description No other bog garden plant will provide as intense a blue as this unusual but very choice wildflower. For this plant to thrive and achieve its full impact, the soil needs to be damp and rich in organic matter and, perhaps most important of all, acid.
Flowers Clusters of rich, deep blue trumpet-shaped flowers appear at the ends of stems during mid- to late summer.
Leaves Lush green, shiny and lance-shaped on short, slender stems.
Cultivation In spring plant in full sun, or light to moderate shade. Mulch with garden compost after planting, and annually each spring. Feed with a general fertilizer at the same time. If the leaves turn yellow in summer, the soil is not acid enough, so water it with sequestered iron to restore the pH levels. This gentian resents disturbance, so leave it well alone once it's established.

Propagation Take softwood cuttings in summer, rooting them in a propagator with slight bottom heat. Seeds can be sown in early spring, again in a propagator, and these should be kept at around 68°F (20°C).
Height Up to 12in (30cm).
Spread Up to 10in (25cm).
Alternative plants The willow gentian (*Gentiana asclepiadea*) produces typical gentian-blue flowers on stems up to 24in (60cm) high, and tolerates some lime in the soil; it also has a white form, 'Alba', and other various pink or pale blue varieties.

ORNAMENTAL RHUBARB (RHEUM PALMATUM)

Type Will survive temperatures down to around 5°F (−15°C).
Origin China.
USDA zone Z6
Description Unlike *Gunnera* (see pages 138–140), which 'pretends' to be an ornamental rhubarb plant, this really is one. Although much smaller than *Gunnera* it is, in its own way, just as dramatic and its leaves combined with the elongated flower heads make this quite an exotic addition to the bog garden.
Flowers During late spring and early summer small, red or purple flowers appear in large plumes on rigid purplish stalks. The stalks can rise to a height of 10ft (3m).
Leaves The leaves are deeply lobed, and are of a rich green or purple (with a reddish tinge to the undersides). Each leaf can be 3ft (90cm) across when mature.
Cultivation Plant in full sun or part-shade, but make sure the soil is moist and rich. Feed with a general fertilizer in spring. Cut down all faded flower heads in late autumn and cover the

ABOVE **With its rhubarb-like leaves, *Rheum palmatum* makes an exotic addition to the bog garden**

dormant crowns with straw or horticultural fleece.
Propagation Divide crowns in spring; plants will need dividing every four or five years.
Height Mature plants can grow up to 6ft (2m) – not including the height of the flower head.
Spread Up to 7ft (2.1m).
Alternative plants *Rheum palmatum rubrum* produces rich, pink flower spikes; 'Atrosanguineum' has red spring leaves, and red flowers in summer; 'Bowles' Crimson' is a deeper red and 'Ace of Hearts' is a miniature version with pink flowers and leaves that are rich red beneath.

PLANTAIN LILIES (*HOSTA* spp.)

Type Fully hardy, surviving temperatures down to around −4°F (−20°C).
Origin China, Japan.
USDA zone Z3–8
Description With more than 70 species and hundreds of modern varieties (which are being added to every year), there are few hardy herbaceous plants that can match the variety, diversity of form, texture and leaf colourings of the hosta. The Chinese *Hosta plantaginea* was the first hosta introduced to European gardens, in the late 1700s, and other varieties quickly followed, mainly from Japan.

ABOVE *Hosta fortunei var. albopicta*

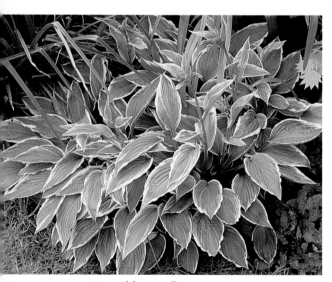

ABOVE *Hosta undulata var. albomarginata*

Hostas are, of course, principally grown for their large, graceful leaves.

Flowers In summer they produce long stems of small, nodding, lily-like flowers in shades of lilac, mauve and purple, as well as a few which are pure white. Some are fragrant.

Leaves The leaves vary in size from those just a few centimetres long, to those the size of dinner plates. Just as the sizes vary, so too do the textures of the leaves, from very smooth, through to shiny, dull, matt and even corrugated. Add to these variables the bewildering array of leaf colours and variegations and one can see why they are one of our most popular plants.

Cultivation Plant in spring, in a position that receives full sun, or dappled shade. Mulch in spring or autumn, and give a handful of general fertilizer per plant in spring. Cut back dead flower stalks as soon as they have faded, and cut or pull away tattered foliage as soon as it starts to look bad. The biggest problem, and famously so, is the attacking of hosta leaves by slugs and snails.

Propagation By division in autumn or spring.

Recommended species Probably the most popular species of hosta is *H. fortunei*, and one of the most attractive forms is *H. fortunei* var. *albopicta*. It has bright yellow leaves distinctively edged with green in spring, which change to all-over green as they age. Meanwhile, *H. fortunei* var. *aureomarginata* has leaves of a rich dark green with a yellow border, and *H. fortunei* var. *hyacintha* has slightly shiny, small green leaves with long points.

Hosta crispula is a great favourite, with striking white-margined broad, pointed dark green leaves. It also offers stems of lilac-purple flowers in mid-summer. *H. decorata* has bold-ribbed leaves with cream margins; the flowers are pale purple. *H. elata* is amongst the earliest varieties to flower, with pale lilac blooms in early summer, held aloft pale green, matt leaves with wavy edges.

Wavy-edged foliage is a characteristic of the varieties of *Hosta undulata*. One of the earliest varieties is *H. undulata* var. *albomarginata* (also seen sometimes named 'Thomas Hogg'); it has a strong creamy-white edge to the leaves.

ABOVE *Primula japonica* produces flowers in several 'candelabra' tiers

PRIMULAS

Type Fully hardy, surviving temperatures down to around −4°F (−20°C).

Origin Worldwide.

USDA zone Z5–7

Description Whichever bog plants you grow, there should always be room for a primula or ten. The primula genus ranks as one of the largest, most variable, durable and likeable of all plant genera. There are primulas for growing in pots, on rockeries, in flower beds, in woodland dells and at the sides of a pond.

Flowers Each flower comprises five lobes fused into a tube, either borne singly or in clusters (whorls) around a leafless stem.

Leaves All species produce a basal rosette of entire to lobed, often hairy leaves.

Cultivation Sunny or lightly shaded places are best, and primulas prefer a fairly rich, organic, slightly acid soil. Mulch lightly around the plants in spring. Cut back dead flower heads and foliage where feasible, and divide the plants every three or four years.

ABOVE *Primula pulverulenta* is a candelabra species with flowers from pale pink to mauve

151

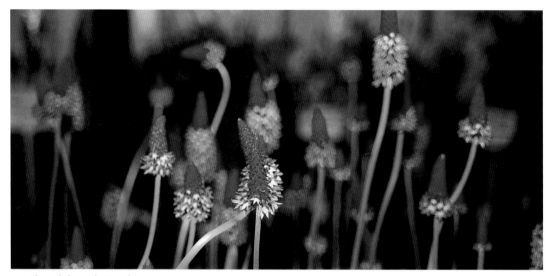

ABOVE **The orchid primula (*P. vialii*)**

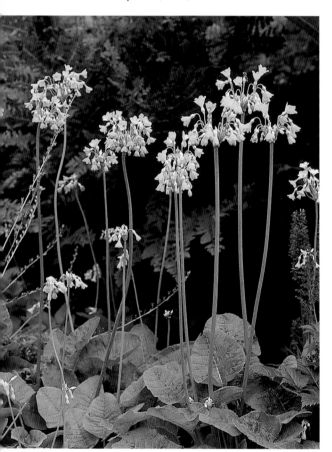

ABOVE **The Himalayan cowslip (*Primula florindae*) is similar to a tall wild cowslip**

Depending on your chosen primulas, you may find that they are susceptible to such garden pests as slugs and snails, viruses, fungal leaf spots and burrowing leaf miner grubs.

Propagation Sow fresh seeds on to the surface of soil-based potting composts under glass in spring. Germination is slow, can be erratic, and some hybrids and strains will not come true from seed (that is, the offspring will not always be identical to the parents). Alternatively, divide mature plants in spring or autumn.

Recommended species Some primulas are temperamental, or elusive, but the following small selection is sure to provide colour and interest if you give them the preferred growing conditions as outlined above.

Primula aurantiaca is one of the so-called candelabra primulas (meaning that, like others, it bears its flowers in rounded clusters, or whorls, at intervals along the main central stem). It has striking orange or orange-red blooms in late spring and early summer, which is slightly earlier than the other candelabras. The flower stems can reach 30in (75cm) in height.

Primula japonica is possibly the best-known candelabra primula, with lush leaves and several tiers of red, pink or white flowers opening at stages throughout early and mid-summer. Four of the best varieties are: 'Alba', white; 'Apple Blossom', pink; 'Miller's Crimson', deep pink; and 'Postford White', white.

Other candelabras include *Primula beesiana*, deep red with yellow centres; *P.* x *bulleesiana*, featuring a wide range of colours from yellow, orange and pink through to red and purple, and *P. pulverulenta*, pale pink or mauve.

The drumstick primula, *P. denticulata*, is extremely popular, with its neat globular pink-purple heads 3in (8cm) across. There are many garden forms, the flower colours of which are generally given away by their varietal names: 'Glenroy Crimson', 'Inshriach Carmine', 'Prichard's Ruby', 'Robinson's Red' and 'Snowball'.

The orchid primula, *P. vialii*, is one of the most stunning of all primula species. It is distinct from the others in that it has startling spikes of bright red buds, and in the early part of the summer the lowest buds open to mauve or lilac blooms. The top buds are the last to open, giving the whole flower head a dual red/lilac combination.

There is little that can beat a patch of Himalayan cowslips, *P. florindae*. This plant resembles a very tall, shaggy cowslip – at around 32in (80cm) on mature specimens – with slightly powdery sulphur yellow flower heads in early summer. A smaller version of the Himalayan cowslip is *P. sikkimensis*, which has its origins in the Chinese marshlands. It has bright yellow flowers in mid-spring.

RODGERSIA (*RODGERSIA AESCULIFOLIA*)

Type Will survive temperatures down to around 5°F (–15°C).
Origin China.
USDA zone Z7
Description This is one of those plants that looks perfect next to a woodland stream or large pond, but incongruous when grown anywhere else in the garden. Its leaves look as if they should be growing high up on a horse chestnut tree (*Aesculus*), but this plant is, of course, a border plant. Lovers of bold, dramatic, architectural plants will adore this.
Flowers In mid-summer, plumes of many tiny pinkish-red blossoms are held well above the foliage.
Leaves Large, shining and rich green, usually evenly suffused reddish bronze. Each palmate leaf has an impressive network of veins.
Cultivation This needs a moist soil if it is to do well. Mulch in the spring and autumn and give a handful of general fertilizer in the spring. Leave the flower heads in place once they are finished as the reddish seedheads come along much later in the season. Do not disturb the plants once they are established.
Propagation Spring divisions of the tough surface rhizomes will soon develop into their own clumps.
Height Up to 5ft (1.5m).
Spread Up to 3ft (1m).
Alternative plants *Rodgersia pinnata* 'Superba' has deeply divided leaves and white flowers; *R. podophylla* has palm-shaped leaves and cream flowers; and *R. sambucifolia* has leaves like an elder, and white flowers.

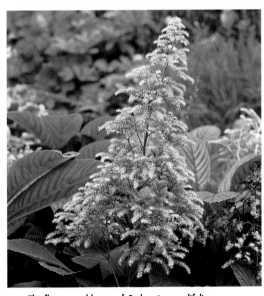

ABOVE **The flowers and leaves of** *Rodgersia aesculifolia*

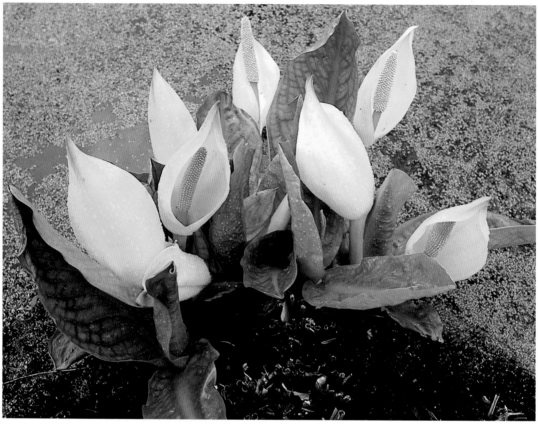

ABOVE **The dramatic – and rather exotic – skunk cabagge (*Lysichiton americanus*)**

SKUNK CABBAGE (*LYSICHITON AMERICANUS*)

Type Will survive temperatures down to around 5°F (–15°C).

Origin The western side of North America.

USDA zone Z6

Description What an unpleasant name for a wonderful plant. When sniffed at close quarters, the heavy aroma produced by the foliage will explain why it is so called. This really is a star of the bog garden, however: its eye-catching golden yellow spathe flowers appear before the large, spectacular leaves. It really pays to grow this next to water, where the reflection can add to the magnificence. You can tell I'm a fan.

Flowers Large, bright yellow spathes in typical arum style; each one can be 12in (30cm) in length and some 8in (20cm) across.

Leaves The leaves are long, rounded and fresh yellow-green. They emerge in summer after the flowers have faded.

Cultivation Plant in spring, 30in (75cm) apart if growing more than one. The soil should be enriched with plenty of organic matter, for these are very hungry plants. The best position is in partial shade, although it likes growing in full sun almost as much. This is a relatively undemanding plant, but it would pay to provide a twice-yearly mulch in spring and autumn. Feed with a general fertilizer in spring. Do not disturb the plants once they are established.

Propagation In late spring or early summer sow fresh seed in moist soil. Self-sown seedlings – which can get out of hand – can be transplanted at any time.

ABOVE **The oriental bog arum (*Lysichiton camschatcensis*) produces white spathes**

Height Up to 3ft (1m).
Spread Up to 2ft (60cm).
Alternative plants This plant is also referred to as the American bog arum, and the botanical name is often spelt wrongly – i.e. *Lysichitum americanum*. A slightly smaller plant is the oriental bog arum (*L. camschatcensis*) which has white spathes.

WATER AVENS (*GEUM RIVALE*)

Type Hardy. Will survive temperatures down to around −4°F (−20°C).
Origin Throughout the northern hemisphere.
USDA zone Z3
Description This is a hardy woodland plant which enjoys a wetter soil than many of its compatriots. It also exists in many cultivated forms with a wide selection of flower colours. It is closely related to the garden geums, but its flowers are much more dainty.

Flowers During late spring and early summer small pinkish-purple bells hang in loose heads on arching, hairy stalks.
Leaves Small, rich green, rounded and slightly toothed at the edges.
Cultivation Plant in spring or autumn in a lightly shaded spot. If planting more than one, set them out 12in (30cm) apart. These plants do not require staking. Mulch in the autumn with moist, well-rotted garden compost. Cut down top-growth in late autumn.
Propagation Divide the plants in autumn or spring (they will need this every third or fourth year anyway).
Height Up to 18in (45cm).
Spread Up to 18in (45cm).
Alternative plants Among the selected forms are 'Album' with white flowers; 'Leonard's Variety', pinkish-orange flowers; and 'Variegatum', with cream marks on the leaves.

155

Glossary

Algae
Non-flowering microscopic plants, mainly aquatic; the reason for pond water turning green.

Amphibian (amphibious)
Creature able to live both on land and in water.

Annual
Plant grown from seed that germinates, flowers, sets seed and dies in one growing year.

Biennial
A plant that grows from seed and completes its life cycle within two years.

Bog garden
An area where the soil is permanently damp, either naturally so or artificially created.

Butyl
Strong waterproof material made from rubber, usually supplied in sheets or by the roll.

Crown
Basal part of a perennial plant where roots and stems join at soil level, and from where new shoots are produced.

Cultivar
A cultivated plant clearly distinguished by one or more characteristics and which retains these characteristics when propagated; a contraction of 'cultivated variety', and often abbreviated to 'cv.' in plant naming.

Dead heading
The removal of spent flowers or flower heads.

Deciduous
Plant that loses its leaves at the end of every growing year, and which renews them at the start of the next.

Double
Referred to in flower terms as a bloom with several layers of petals; usually there would be a minimum of 20 petals. 'Very double' flowers have more than 40 petals.

Genus (pl. Genera)
A category in plant naming, comprising a group of related species.

Head
The height of a water outlet above the level of a lower pool.

Header pool
The uppermost pool in a recirculating water feature.

Hybrid
The offspring of genetically different parents, usually produced in cultivation, but occasionally arising in the wild.

Leaching
Loss of nutrients from the topsoil, carried downwards by water.

Marginal plant
Plants that grow partially submerged in shallow water or in boggy soil at the water's edge.

Mulch
Layer of material applied to the soil surface, to conserve moisture, improve its structure, protect roots from frost, and suppress weeds.

Oxygenator
Submerged aquatic plant, the leaves and stems of which release oxygen into the water as a by-product of photosynthesis.

Perennial
Plant that lives for at least three seasons.

Photosynthesis
The process of food manufacture in plants, whereby chlorophyll in leaves traps the sun's

energy, combines it with carbon dioxide in the air and hydrogen in water and creates carbohydrates.

pH scale
A scale measured from 1 to 14 that indicates the alkalinity or acidity of soil: pH 7 is neutral; pH 1–7 is acid; pH 7–14 is alkaline.

Rhizome
A specialized, usually horizontally creeping, swollen or slender underground stem that acts as a storage organ, producing shoots along its length.

Root-ball
The roots and surrounding soil or compost visible when a plant is removed from a pot.

Sideshoot
A stem that arises from the side of a main shoot or stem.

Single
In flower terms, a single layer of petals opening out into a fairly flat shape, comprising no more than five petals.

Spathe
A large leaf-like structure that encloses or surrounds the flower of certain plants, such as those of the Arum family.

Species
A category in plant naming, the rank below genus, containing related, individual plants.

Sucker
Generally a shoot that arises from below ground, emanating from a plant's roots, but also refers to any shoot on a grafted plant that originates from below the graft union.

Variety
Botanically, a naturally occurring variant of a wild species; usually shortened to 'var.' in plant naming.

About the author

Graham Clarke was born into gardening – literally. His father was in charge of the world-famous Regent's Park in London and at the time of Graham's birth the family lived in a lodge within the public gardens there. During his formative years Graham was surrounded by quality horticulture, so it was little surprise when he chose this as his career. He went to study with England's Royal Horticultural Society at Wisley Gardens, and after that worked as a gardener at Buckingham Palace in London. This very private garden is seen by Her Majesty the Queen on most of the days she is in residence.

For more than 20 years Graham has been a gardening writer and journalist. He has written eight books, and countless articles for most of the major UK gardening magazines. He has been the editor of *Amateur Gardening* (the UK's leading weekly magazine for amateurs) and *Horticulture Week* (the UK's leading weekly magazine for professionals), and is now a freelance garden writer and consultant. He lives in Dorset, on England's south coast, with his wife and two daughters.

Index

Pages highlighted in **bold** indicate photographs of plants.

INDEX

GMC Publications Ltd, 166 High Street, Lewes, East Sussex BN7 1XU, United Kingdom
Tel: 01273 488005 Fax: 01273 402866
www.gmcbooks.com

Contact us for a complete catalogue, or visit our website.